Embracing
a Beautiful
GOD

Fritz

May Beautiful blessings
enfold you always

Patricia Adam Farmer

Embracing
a Beautiful
GOD

PATRICIA ADAMS FARMER

CHALICE
PRESS
ST. LOUIS, MISSOURI

Bible quotations, unless otherwise noted, are from the *New Revised Standard Version Bible*, copyright 1989, Division of Christian Education of the National Council of the Churches of Christ in the United States of America. Used by permission. All rights reserved.

Cover photo: Ron Dauer
Cover and interior design: Elizabeth Wright
Art direction: Elizabeth Wright

This book is printed on acid-free, recycled paper.

Visit Chalice Press on the World Wide Web at
www.chalicepress.com

10 9 8 7 6 5 4 3 2 1   03 04 05 06 07 08

Library of Congress Cataloging–in–Publication Data

Farmer, Patricia Adams.
    Embracing a beautiful God / Patricia Adams Farmer.
    p. cm.
Includes indexes.
    ISBN 0-8272-0818-9
1. Spiritual life—Christianity. I. Title.
    BV4501.3 .F37 2003
    242—dc21

                                                2002152174

Printed in the United States of America

For Ron,
my co-conspirator in the search
for all that is Good and True and Beautiful

CONTENTS

PART 5
Embracing Beauty in Cats and Other Creatures

FOREWORD

This is one of those rare books that *is* what it is *about:* Beauty. In poetic images, Patricia Farmer invites us into her own reveries about God and the world. Her theme is a theology of beauty, of finding inspiration—and consternation!—in the small, ordinary things of daily life.

While this inspiring book draws us into the simple beauties of a sandy beach, of a lovely path, of deeply satisfying personal relationships, it neither hides ugliness nor paints for us a utopian world. Rather, beauty for Patricia Farmer is holding the contrasting tensions of the good, bad, and indifferent together in such a way that transformation can occur. We are taken not only into the beauty of a meditative moment but also into the ugliness of a consumer society gone amok, of corporate greed, of terrible conflict. What are we, as ordinary individuals, to do with such facts about our world? Farmer suggests that we can live into the tension created by the contrast between these ugly facts and the more wondrous side of existence. This tension itself can inspire us to act for transformation of the negative into more positive ways of communal being. The beauty found in meditating on the lovely provides a stark contrast to the negative elements of greed and guns. This contrast pushes us toward the work of creating beauty in our social lives. And while our actions may seem like small deeds in our personal and communal living, the interdependence of our world is such that every action invites a reaction. We can be agents toward beauty; our efforts matter.

Interdependence is the major supposition of Farmer's work. She is a process theologian who thinks and lives from the basic reality that all things and people and events are interconnected. God's work in this interrelatedness is always toward the production of beauty, taking up what is and nurturing it toward what it yet might be. Our own openness to beauty is at the same time an openness to God, answering the divine invitation to participate more fully in God's creative work.

Beauty, then, is not just a happenstance of the universe, not some totally subjective construal dependent wholly upon human imagination. Is a sunset beautiful whether we see it or not? In Farmer's world, yes. Is this strange and awesome confluence of green and blue that makes up our planet just incidentally beautiful? Or was it only beautiful when we saw it so from space photographs? In Farmer's world, this planet is intentionally beautiful. Beauty is not some side benefit invented by human perception. Rather, beauty is at the heart of all things. Beauty is at the heart of God, and the beauty that we see—and even create—is like the trailing wake from God's hand across the ocean of the universe. This is why, in attending to beauty, we become open to the mystery of God. In attending to beauty, we open ourselves to participation in God's own transformation of things to modes of beauty not yet realized, but hovering still on the edges of becoming.

So take a "Beauty break," as Patricia Farmer puts it, and wander into these words that wait for you. You will go beneath the surface of things, and come up with new wisdom in your own daily participation in beauty.

Marjorie Hewitt Suchocki

ACKNOWLEDGMENTS

I am most grateful to my husband, Ron Farmer, who nudged me to the point of annoyance to have these philosophical ponderings published. He said that I should either publish them or open a philosophy shop and dispense them like Lucy's advice in *Peanuts*. The philosophy shop was too expensive.

I am enormously grateful to David Polk, Editor-in-Chief of Chalice Press, for believing in this project.

I am also indebted to those philosophers and theologians whose writings, teachings, and friendship have influenced the formation of my own worldview, especially John B. Cobb, Jr., David Ray Griffin, and Marjorie Hewitt Suchocki of the Claremont School of Theology.

Thank you to fellow writing friends Robert and Adrienne Brizee, Jay B. McDaniel, Bruce G. Epperly, and Anna Rollins for reading my manuscript and to Rabbi Harold Kushner for showing me how to write about God with the courage of one's experience.

Finally, I want to thank my mother, Ruth Schwartz Adams, who shuttled me from dance lessons to art lessons to music lessons, and who always made me learn my spelling words.

PROLOGUE

Just One Thing

After the feet of beauty fly my own.

EDNA ST. VINCENT MILLAY

I have come to realize in my years of pondering and praying and philosophizing over both the mundane dailiness of experience and the catastrophic evils of the world that there is only one thing worth all our effort. Just one thing. And it is more of a joy than an effort. That is because we are born with an urge to do it, an innate, divine yearning to do this one thing. That mysteriously imbedded urge to which we must give ourselves over, wholly, is this: *to embrace the beautiful in each moment.*

We live in difficult times, bearing a heavy shadow of war, fear, injustice, and religious fanaticism, which makes this divine urge implanted in us all the more urgent. If we desire the world to be transformed for the better, we need to begin where we are with a philosophy of life and a view of God that can contribute to this creative transformation. Violence begets violence; only Beauty can transform evil at its roots.

Beauty, as a philosophical concept, is rather mysterious–a slippery elf, hard to catch hold of, impossible to define. But let me try anyway: *Beauty is that which glistens on the edges of our yearnings and lures us into the depth of things.* Its mystery lures us to deep communion with all creation. Its sensuality calls us to incarnate God on our walks on a sandy beach. Its glistening lends buoyancy to heavy days.

I will offer pictures and little snatches of how I believe Beauty works in the world, but it's only true Beauty if you experience it for yourself and define it with your own experience.

One thing I have learned in my search for the beautiful is that we know it when we see it. It comes to us like a revelation, like grace, like two snow-white kittens dropping out of heaven on a

Sunday morning, landing in a cardboard box on the steps of a church with a sign "Adopt Me." Beauty happens, and we know it when we see it. And when we see it, we fall madly in love.

This is a book of little stories and lessons that Beauty has taught me—a "philosophy of beauty" spun out of the simple threads of daily life. It is intended to help you embrace beautiful possibilities even in the most tragic of times. My wish is that you catch a glimpse of your deeper connections within the colorful tapestry of the world and discover a beautiful God underneath all those beastly pictures of divinity that have wounded so many of us. And in this spacious and tender place I pray you will allow yourself to be enfolded in the fullness of Beauty's gifts: love, creativity, joy, forgiveness, courage, compassion, enchantment, serenity, and faith for coping and transcending whatever challenges you face in this unsettling world of ours.

These stories and lessons are born out of many strands of experience in my variegated journey as a philosopher, a teacher, a minister, a musician, and a writer. But mostly, these are simple lessons Beauty has taught me in my honest—but often painfully awkward—trial-and-error attempts at living. I invite you to embrace Beauty with me and linger long enough to get a glimpse of a God who nourishes Beauty in the world.

Anne Morrow Lindbergh says, "Every person, especially every woman, should be alone sometime during the year—some part of each week, and each day." That is because "certain springs are tapped only when we are alone."[1] I have discovered that the best way to wrap my life around the power of Beauty is to take Lindbergh's advice to heart in a once-a-week "Beauty Break." Not a trip to the salon, but a retreat to a place that nourishes inner beauty, a quiet place with a book and a writing pad and perhaps even a bar of chocolate.

Alone. Once a week. This works, I have discovered, even if it is only for a couple of hours. There is a sense of renewal, of getting one's bearings again. You may wish to take this book with you on such a day and focus on one story—either in sequence or using the thematic index to match your needs—using each story as a simple proposal for your own philosophizing; a prelude to prayer; a

---

[1] Anne Morrow Lindbergh, *Gift from the Sea* (New York: Pantheon Books, 1955), 48–50.

springboard for your own discoveries, writings, art work, homilies, or journaling.

So let us be alone at least once each week to do this one thing. Let us practice embracing Beauty in those solitary moments, that it might carry us through the week and transform our days. Let us pray and dream and imagine ourselves as we know we can be, and a world liberated from poverty, oppression, fear, and violence. We have nothing more powerful to contribute during these unsettling days than to nurture Beauty and protect it fiercely in our hearts.

PART 1

Embracing Beauty in Creation and Cocreation

Beauty is merely the Spiritual making itself known sensuously.

G. W. F. HEGEL,
THE PHILOSOPHY OF RELIGION

Caught in the Lure

One is forced against one's mind, against all tidy resolutions,
back into the primeval rhythms of the seashore.

ANNE MORROW LINDBERGH

When I'm suddenly overcome with that "heavy laden" feeling that makes me want to crawl into a hole and escape from the world, that's exactly what I do. I escape. We all need our escape routes, and mine is the road that winds down to the rocky beach near my home.

Today is Presidents' Day. George Washington and Abraham Lincoln have thankfully graced some of us with a day off and all of us with sunshine—and the kind of air that wraps around your skin like silk. I find my place on the sandy beach, kick off my sandals, and walk down to the playful water's edge. The teasing surf overtakes my feet as I'm drawn into the chilly thrill of the Pacific Ocean. The rolling breakers wash away my crusty edges, leaving me smooth and soft and cool, like the wet sand between my toes.

Salty spray—delicious on my lips—cleanses all the accumulated junk that clings to me. Here I am, drawn inward as if there is no world outside of this place. Here beauty illumines all faces, people of all sizes, colors, ages, intelligence, economic worth, degrees of physical attraction—all this is leveled out. Everyone is simply a shining being, and everyone is beautiful. It's true—the sea does that, especially when the sun is generous. The presence of divine Beauty levels everything out and releases us from categories and competition.

Children shine with a special brightness by the sunny seashore, chasing gulls, chasing one another. Grandpa takes his tiny twin grandchildren into the surf, each little girl holding on for dear life to granddad's huge hands. Grandma, plump and well-protected with a wide-brim hat, stands by with camera in hand. I see her shining too. No one escapes the luminous pull of sunshine and sea. It just overtakes you as a monster wave does. No one has a chance of escaping into cynicism today.

Grandpa's gentleness with the little ones moves me. My eyes rest on the radiant beings on either side of him, jumping around like flapping fishes caught in the lure and reeled in.

A middle-aged man with neat hair and wrap-around sunglasses runs by with a red kite. He's with no one, just himself. He's shining like the others, not dreary faced with worry over unpredictable clients and job deadlines. He's playing in the sun and is himself one of the happy victims of Beauty's joy. It is as if we are all caught in this lure, flapping around with a joy that is primal and simple, as it is with children.

Alfred North Whitehead says that God is "the lure for feeling, the eternal urge of desire." I understand this today in a fresh way. God is like the alluring ocean on a bright day, compelling us to abandon everything but who we really are. When all the crustiness is washed off, we are simply shining beings flying kites and holding tiny hands and jumping like fishes.

Restless, rolling, mysterious—God is the ever-moving continuity and freshness of the sea, never the same in any moment. God's heartbeat is like the rhythm of the ocean, and when we succumb to this alluring force, we cannot be anything less than shining beings on the edge of a playful universe.

Arise, shine; for your light has come.
ISAIAH 60:1

The Mislaid Egg

A woman is like a tea bag; you don't know her strength until she is in hot water.

ELEANOR ROOSEVELT

Surviving a woman's purse can be daunting. Especially if you are an egg. Although hard to believe, I unknowingly carried a raw egg—very large and very raw—in my purse for three days. Three days of tossing my purse around. Three days of slinging my purse over my shoulder. Three days of digging through my purse looking for my keys.

Then, on the third day of slinging, tossing, and digging, the egg surfaced. Untouched. Pure. Not even a crack.

It's not hard to explain—how the egg got into the purse, that is. I was visiting a friend who had hens on her property. I inquired about these chickens who ran around clucking happily through the grass. I commented on the value of free-range eggs. She disappeared and then reappeared, proudly displaying a huge, magnificent brown egg and put it in my hands. I thanked her, putting the egg half-consciously into my purse, where I put everything else.

Later in the week when this unassuming, free-range specimen peered back at me from my purse, I naturally gasped. "Disaster averted!" I thought. What would my purse have looked like if I had not been so lucky? Say I was at a posh restaurant and reached in to pull out my billfold to pay the bill and then… Or, more likely, I would be checking out at the grocery store, and while whipping out my Visa card, out comes a whipped egg instead. All these things ran through my mind in an instant before I settled back to breathe a prayer of thanksgiving for small miracles and hardy free-range eggs.

Perhaps it was my guardian angel that kept that egg whole and happy in its fragile little shell. Or just dumb luck, which is more likely.

I thought about that egg for a long time, the miracle of its survival in the dark, chaotic abyss of my purse. Eggs are fragile. People are fragile too. But perhaps we are hardier than we think. Even when we are tossed about and abused in every way, we can survive. The egg tells us that we can take a lot of abuse and still not crack.

We often get tossed and slung about by situations beyond our control. Sometimes we survive. Sometimes we crack. And there are times when our fragility is painfully and outrageously demonstrated. On September 11, 2001, we found out that neither flesh nor steel is invulnerable. Things do break, die, crack, and tumble down, and we are left with deep chasms of pain in our souls.

The egg in my purse was lucky. This time. But in the very nature of things, the most precious things perish. My favorite philosopher, Alfred North Whitehead, sees this "perpetual perishing" as the very nature of reality. However, he also says that each moment in time perishes and yet "lives forever more."

Even if our physical bodies give way to death, for reasons beyond our control, we still survive in those we leave behind and in God's eternal care. "On the third day" Jesus survived, transcending his own death in a new form of existence. His vulnerability was only physical. Spiritually, he was a giant with a soul that refused to crack.

We are like that too–full of something strong and hardy and shimmering, with a brilliance that will not be dimmed or damned.

Even if we crack.

Beauty loves such fragile things as fresh brown eggs and newborn kittens and antique china cups. We find Beauty hiding out in such fragile places as forests and bird sanctuaries and waters where dolphins play. And we find Beauty mostly in people and in the way they make our hearts leap when they smile at us. All this is to be cherished, protected, and loved.

Beauty is at once fragile and strong, perishing in time.

Yet it lives forever more.

God is our refuge and strength,
a very present help in trouble.
PSALM 46:1

English Garden

Once in a golden hour,
I cast to earth a seed.
Up there came a flower,
the people said a weed.

ALFRED, LORD TENNYSON

There is a time for harmony, and there is a time for disharmony.

My Liverpudlian friends, Alison and Philip, sent me 4 x 6" glossy photos of their English garden. When I opened the mail, I was dazzled! Yellow tulips, red poppies, pink geraniums, purple periwinkles, and climbing wisteria–all growing together in untamed liveliness and enchanting disorder.

One thing Alison and Philip have taught me about these English "cottage gardens'" is that there is no orderly, formal pattern or defined way of doing things. It's not like having high tea with scones and cream and lumps of sugar and pieces of silver in their proper place. The English garden is quite different from all that is "just so" in English life.

In fact, famous English gardener Christopher Lloyd loves to tease the followers of garden fashion by overturning their notions of the correctness of certain colors together. He might shock them by placing magenta alongside orange to achieve the desired effect. Or he might even mix vegetables and flowers in the same garden! Yes, the English love their cottage gardens and the untidiness of things growing together in unorthodox patterns and hodgepodge variety.

I am intrigued with the concept of a cottage garden. It is honest. It mirrors the way things are. The colors, variety, and textures of life just spring up willy-nilly. No matter how hard we try to match perfectly the colors and place the seeds just so, something unexpected always pops up.

We tend our gardens. We want our gardens to be perfect, especially in comparison with our neighbor's garden. That's the way we are trained to think. But who says that our gardens have to be flawless and perfectly pleasing to all who pass by? A few unusual clashes of color and contrasts of texture might just splash things up a bit.

A few eyebrows raised, now and then, is a good thing.

Having to have things just so, with no tolerance for novelty or imperfection, is the opposite of a cottage garden, and the opposite of a beautiful life. We are planted and nurtured by a God who lavishes upon the world a good measure of untamed Beauty.

Divine Beauty teases us at times with unheard-of, crazy, mismatched, and even shocking possibilities! We might just want to throw aside our primrose path of expectations and entertain a bit of nonconformity for the love of novelty, for the joy of adventure. For the sake of Beauty.

What if we made room in our all-too-formal lives for a little patch of garden that is not planned out or designed to perfection? What if we allowed for a little unorthodoxy here and there? A dash of imperfection.

A little wildness.

You may be tending a common notion that you are too old or too poor or too busy to go back to school. Or that you are not talented enough to be a painter or writer. Or not courageous enough to try out for the part in the community theatre. Or simply afraid to put a bit a Tabasco in your scrambled eggs. So everything is planned with fastidious neatness and security systems in place, but with no real adventure. No real risk.

Maybe you need to think more about English gardens. Maybe you need to explore the wildness within your garden before you close off your dreams into more commonsensical plans. Perhaps if you let just a few feral notions into your head, you will want to go skydiving or learn to play the harp. Or write a book. Or maybe even fall in love.

A beautiful life is not chaotic, but it allows for a certain amount of chaos. If we don't allow for this, we begin tearing out "weeds" that might in fact be flowers. We lose the freshness and zest that we are meant to enjoy and cultivate.

We do violence to things for the sake of perfection.

Some of us need more novelty than others, but we all need a measure of untidiness within the harmony of our lives. We need to tap into Beauty's cottage garden style at least in some corner of our being.

Once in a golden hour we need to plant seeds of novelty alongside the ordinary, seeds of freshness up against the run-of-the-mill, and a few seeds of wildness scattered here and there. Then we might just wake up one spring morning to discover that Beauty has finally bloomed at our house.

And even the birds are enchanted.

> *My beloved has gone down to his garden,*
> *to the beds of spices,*
> *to pasture his flock in the gardens,*
> *and to gather lilies.*
> SONG OF SOLOMON 6:2

Sprawling Mermaid

Tell me, brother, What are we?
Spirits bathing in the sea
Of Deity.

CHRISTOPHER CRANCH

The sea is my sanctuary. I come here to listen, observe, and sift out a moment of grace to take back home. Today is gorgeous. The soft, dreamy stretches of sea move out into a blue infinity, calling me to linger, reflect, and ponder the divine offerings of this moment.

The very sight of the sea has a way of making one think huge thoughts, deep thoughts, swirling thoughts. You can't help it.

It is a numinous moment. My imagination is stirring, let loose by the ocean spray. I want to be part of this massive, fierce Beauty—so mysterious and powerful—and learn of its deep secrets.

I sit down on a bench that is much more than a wooden bench overlooking the ocean. It is also a work of art entitled "Support." On the back of the bench, two stone figures support each side of the bench as if holding the whole thing together. Underneath is another stone figure—this one on its back—pushing upward, supporting the bench from below. The invitation is just too alluring not to accept. I sit down, feeling quite supported by my stone friends.

What I want to do—but would never dare—is to sprawl out on this bench like a vagrant and let the sun drench me for hours on end. Sometimes that's all we want—just to stretch out in the nurturing sun, supported by something strong and caring. We want the feeling of solidness underneath us so that while we're dreaming half awake in the sun, our support won't be pulled out from under us. Things do get pulled out from under us, don't they? Jobs, friendships, love, health, wealth, a sense of being safe in the world.

We want safety, yes.

Other times, we long for adventure, but we're afraid to try this new thing because we wonder if we'll be supported. We're always torn between security and adventure. Which path should we follow?

Perhaps the sea has some answers.

Because I'm still sitting, not sprawling, I have a perfect view of the sea and rocks. First I notice the high tide and the choppy, restless sea below. Then I notice the rocks–huge, solid, shining as they rise up out of the sea with immovable dignity. My first thought is this: While this contrast makes for a striking picture postcard view, it also suggests the nature of a beautiful life. A beautiful life is one that is balanced with both intense, spontaneous feeling and solid, rational wisdom. Taking one over the other impoverishes the whole person, leaving one either chaotically thrashed about or banal, calculating, lifeless.

Where is God in this picture? We might think that God is the solid rock, because our hymns tell us "all other ground is sinking sand." And yes, God is the solid rock; but God is also the mysterious, numinous, groaning sea, in which schools of fish and sea life dance. God is moving about, loving and suffering, living and dying, and gloriously alive to the moment–while also being a solid, unwavering presence who is eternally there for us. Only in this divine balance, both resting in God's strength and flung out in God's joy, can we experience true Beauty.

Sitting here with the supportive stone people, I envision the sea roaring in its overwhelming intensity, so much that even the sea life is wondering if it will survive.

Then I see her.

Out of the swirling chaos, a luminous mermaid appears and perches herself on the largest rock. She is now sprawling out on the rock (as I would like to do on this bench), and with her shiny fin flapping away in the sun, she leans back to feel the warm solid rock at her back.

She is taking a coffee break of sorts from the foamy, churning sea. It's lovely to be in the sea, with all its mystery and surprises, but even the mermaid needs a moment of stillness in the sun with a solid rock at her back.

We are like the mermaid, created both for the adventure of the sea and the safety of the rock. We are gloriously a part of it all!

The sea is passionate, teeming with life and mystery. The rock is assuredly steady, not minding the stirring sea pounding it on all sides, constantly and sometimes ferociously. It just sits there as serenely as Buddha himself, ready for mermaids and wayfarers to steady themselves on its solidness. God is the sea and the rock, the energy and the calm, the fragile life and the enduring strength. God lures us to balance ourselves among the contrasts, mirroring God's own Beauty. Never clinging fearfully to the rock or flailing about in the chaotic sea, we can sprawl out with joyful abandon and know that we are always and forever *supported*.

> *For he will hide me in his shelter...he will set me high on a rock.*
> PSALM 27:5

Getting There

There are no shortcuts to any place worth going.
BEVERLY SILLS

A road trip south to see the famous "Flower Fields" of Carlsbad, California, sounded like the perfect Saturday afternoon getaway. A well-meaning friend at lunch–the friend everyone has, who knows everything about everything–gave me instructions for the perfect afternoon of flowers, lunch, and sight-seeing. So I had her write down her vast wealth of knowledge on the back of a napkin, and plans were set.

What could be more delightful than a road trip such as this one? Plenty. Going to the dentist might have been more fun, at least in the beginning.

First was the horrific traffic jam. With little or no compassion for whomever or whatever was making me miss the flower fields, I was neither patient nor kind. "Who is the idiot who caused this?" My husband, knowing that there was no safe way to counter irrational comments, fiddled with the radio to try to get some traffic information. My only solace was the chocolate I had hidden in my purse, in case of emergency. It seemed as if hours went by before we finally passed the crumpled cars.

Oh, I felt bad. Very, very bad.

Then came getting lost. We drove from one end of Carlsbad to the other looking for the restaurant that was supposed to be

14

"phenomenal" and "famous." We stopped and asked several people; no one had even heard of it. Cranky, hungry (I had depleted my chocolate stash back in the traffic jam), and tired of sitting for hours in the car (my back was killing me), we at least found our way to the flower fields.

Then came the last straw. I was hoping for at least a decent bathroom, but at the entrance there were only outdoor toilets and no running water—wet soap, which I liberally used, but no running water. My husband's experience was no better. So there we go, two sour-faced, soapy, hungry, irritable people, walking through the gate and into the flower fields.

And everything changed.

A couple of sullen tourists—who were beginning to think the whole trip was just a cruel joke concocted in the sinister mind of a know-it-all friend—suddenly forgot the traffic jam, the backaches, the hunt for food, and the soapy hands.

What lay before us pushed everything else aside. Colors, colors, colors! They overwhelmed our senses. Colors dancing in the wind— striking reds, yellows, whites, oranges. Colors filling our senses to the brim with pure delight. Colors just playing in the sunshine as far as we could see. I realized at that moment that the Beauty of God is worth our patience, our endurance, and a lot of irritating circumstances.

When Beauty finally waylays us, we are dumbfounded, repentant, and open to the reality of something greater than ourselves. I'm thankful that my husband and I didn't give up, kill each other, or turn around and go home sulking. We did stick it out to the end, and we were rewarded.

It is this way with our dreams. We dream of something wildly desirable we want in life—a special love, an accomplishment, a home, perhaps a child. Maybe even world peace, or at least a new library in our community. But it may not be "a bed of roses" getting there. Getting where we want to go may take patience and fortitude and perseverance and a good deal of compassion for ourselves and others. And we may not get there at all, but instead land in some other place, a better place that we didn't know existed—a kind of divine serendipity.

Beauty is the lure of God that urges us onward to our dreams, even though the trip is sometimes irksome and often painful. Like

Odysseus making his way back home to Ithaca to his beloved Penelope, the journey to our hope is filled with innumerable obstacles. While giants and evil spells and tempestuous seas may threaten to undo us at every turn, we must stay the course as nobly as we can and find meaning in the journey itself.

Make Beauty your destination, above all. And make sure your dreams are not just for your own welfare but for the well-being of all. Otherwise, when you arrive, you will be deeply disappointed. That is because Beauty enfolds all the colors of creation in her vast field of dreams. Ultimately, our destination is God's own spacious heart–a gracious, welcoming place where all our yearnings can forever dance in splendor. When our goal is set on Beauty, to embrace it above all else, we will find as did Meister Eckhart that "the path is beautiful and pleasant and joyful and familiar."

> *Let us run with perseverance the race that is set before us, looking to Jesus the pioneer and perfecter of our faith, who for the sake of the joy that was set before him endured the cross, disregarding its shame, and has taken his seat at the right hand of the throne of God.*
> HEBREWS 12:1–2

Diamonds on the Water

The image of God's nature is best conceived...of a tender care that nothing be lost.

ALFRED NORTH WHITEHEAD

The sun kisses the water in silver shimmers. I stand here at the edge of the sea, in the clear, warm tide pool, ravished by the silvery light–reminding me that "God is light." I have come to the beach today with mixed feelings of fear and joy, longing for some divine word to weave these thoughts and feelings into a coherent whole. My day alone at the beach lends itself to prayer with eyes wide open.

I say to God, "Right in this moment, I feel so much gratitude for everything I see and feel: the salty air, the shimmering diamonds on the water, the graceful pelican overhead, children running after seagulls, the sense of being alone with all this. I think of my cat who is growing more precious as he nears the end of his life, my husband's love, my dear friends, my work, and this very beach, my sanctuary of tranquility." I go on with a list of everything for which I'm grateful, each thought that brings me joy.

But then I stop smiling.

"But you see, God," I pray, "Here is my dilemma; here is what makes my heart burst and ache at the same time. These things with which I am completely enchanted are ephemeral. Friends come and go, cats die, jobs change, our bodies wear out, even the sand I see today will be different tomorrow. I am afraid to love or find too much joy in things, because everything I adore in life is so fragile and impermanent. How am I to bathe myself in this light of yours when the very sun that makes these shimmering diamonds on the water will be gone in a few hours?"

And somewhere deep down I hear God say to me, "The gifts I offer you do perish, yet each moment of their existence lives on eternally in me, even this moment of watching the dancing light on the water. What makes you ache for Beauty is this very knowledge that everything perishes. Embracing the very terror of this knowledge draws you to Beauty's deepest blessings. So yes, ephemeral—yet forever. Nothing is lost in my eternal care.

"Embrace the perishing world; let yourself go into the alluring light. Your embrace of it makes it come alive! You can let go of the need for permanence when you realize that your experiences of enchantment are saved for eternity and will enrich not only heaven but earth as well. You can let go when you know that things that perish are not in themselves to be worshiped. They are a reflection of me, just as the silver light on the water is a reflection of the sun.

"If you were to chase the light on the water and try to gather all those diamonds in your hand, you could not. Enjoy the shimmering light, and let it be what it is, a reflection of the sun.

"This glistening on the surface is meant to lure you into the depth of things—into your deepest self, into glimpses of eternity, and into deep communion with creation. Your letting go to Beauty will result in gratitude, the kind of contagious joy that will add something of value to all that is."

"God," I say smiling, as the water now laps up to my knees, "I commit myself wholeheartedly to a life of gratitude and a love of enchantment. I will not be afraid to give myself over to these lovely diamonds on the sea, even though they will be gone shortly. The moment is savored for eternity, and you are the source of its radiance. I offer you this moment of gratitude for your eternal care."

The day ends, just as expected. The sun goes down; the diamonds disappear.

But my heart is still smiling.

The sun shall no longer be your light by day,
nor for brightness shall the moon
  give light to you by night;
but the LORD *will be your everlasting light,*
  and your God will be your glory.
ISAIAH 60:19

Panning for Gold

Keep what is worth keeping...
and with a breath of kindness, blow the rest away.

DINAH MULOCK CRAIK

In the sixth grade, Mrs. Spenner had us reenact the California gold rush. We pretended we were the forty-niners who headed west in search of riches, panning endlessly on the river for a little gleam in the dust. We panned for gold right there in the classroom. But the best we ever got was called "fool's gold." It looked pretty and shiny, but it wasn't the real thing. That may have been the most interesting lesson in all of sixth grade. And for this sixth grader, it was only the beginning.

Through the years I have panned for gold in other ways, trying to sift out what is true and good and pure and beautiful. Doing graduate work in philosophy was one of the ways I panned for gold. Studying theology was another. Delving more deeply into the arts enriched the whole realm of my experience. In all these places I found my share of fool's gold, yes, but I found the real thing too. In the spirit of a true forty-niner, each new find only impassioned my search.

But no matter how beautiful or rich or ineffable the thoughts and feelings, I knew something was still missing.

So I continued to pan and sift and search for something more. This time, instead of panning through books, I began to meditate. In meditation I discovered a way of letting things be and letting things go without a lot of fanfare and drama. Life took on more peacefulness and clarity. It was during this time of developing daily habits of meditation and other forms of daily prayer that I began to find a practical spirituality, one that integrated all my knowledge and experiences into a joyful way of being in the world.

While mining this contemplative way of being day by day, I stumbled on the mother lode of riches, the gold mine of happiness. I discovered gratitude.

Gratitude changes my moods, my attitude, my vision of the world around me. But it doesn't come naturally for me. I find it has to be a regular spiritual practice in order to deeply permeate my inner world.

Gratitude is simply panning for the gleam of pure gold in each day. It's shaking things out, gleaning our experience, sorting out the treasures from the junk, keeping what is truly worth cherishing, and dumping out what is not. Gratitude is a way of recreating the world. When we give ourselves over to this practice, we uncover gleams of Beauty that transform the world around us as well as our private moods. This may be simple, but it is enormously significant. Gratitude actually enriches the life of God in the world!

Through this simple process that happens inside our skin, we become panning partners with the Divine, moving things always toward the richest possibilities for wholeness and well-being in the world. It begins inside, but it quickly enriches everything we touch in our world.

Gratitude is Beauty's golden gleam.

How do we find this golden gleam? In her popular book *Simple Abundance,* Sarah Ban Breathnach suggests using a "gratitude journal." I tried it at a time when the world seemed to be a gigantic pain in the neck. A heavy, gray, mushy feeling with sharp, cynical edges threatened to overtake my buoyant spirit. So one night, in desperation, I started a gratitude journal and began sifting for gold.

I sifted every night, no matter how ungrateful I felt. I scooped up the day and searched for that golden gleam. I found little bitty gems, such as "My cat made me laugh today," or "The daffodils are in bloom!" On less generous days, I would write, "The dinner, burned beyond recognition, gave me the opportunity to try out that new Chinese food delivery service." Or on days that were utterly bleak, I simply wrote, "I am alive." And that was enough.

Another way to practice gratitude is to use the time of drifting off to sleep to "count your blessings" in a childlike way. This elegant way to drift off to sleep has as its rewards energy and refreshment in the morning.

And then there is the gratitude walk, walking in Beauty's golden gleam, sharing gratitude with the birds and the sunshine. The time spent in any form of gratitude practice is centered on gem searching. This means letting everything in. All thoughts and feelings are worthy of observation. Nothing should be dumped out without at least a look. Who knows? There may be gold in all that muck that just entered your head! Let everything in. Just don't keep everything.

Find the gem, enfold it with gratitude, and "with a breath of kindness, blow the rest away." This is panning for gold. This practice is part of a contemplative lifestyle, a way of prayer, a shining path to Beauty's door.

Finally, beloved, whatever is true, whatever is honorable, whatever is just, whatever is pure, whatever is pleasing, whatever is commendable, if there is any excellence and if there is anything worthy of praise, think about these things.
PHILIPPIANS 4:8

Gathering Up

We have seething through us the creativity that built the stars.
BRIAN SWIMME

Lenora is a ballroom dancer. She is Greek, gregarious, gorgeous, and always the belle of the ball. But to balance her active social life, she carves out time to work in her flower garden, creating stunning arrangements from her labors. She welcomes spring with a vase of happy daffodils on her kitchen table. In summer she goes wild, filling her home with vases of colorful snapdragons, Shasta daisies, bellflowers, golden yarrow, black-eyed Susans, and anything else in bloom at the time. In the center of her solarium, Lenora reserves one elegant crystal vase for sunflowers, because in her words, "they are cheerful and signify the epitome of summer's golden days." Lenora plays with color, scent, and texture in solitary bliss simply to feed her soul and bathe her world in Beauty.

We may not be gardeners or even own a flower pot, but we need time each week to gather up the scattered pieces of ourselves and create something for the sake of Beauty. Nothing fancy or high-pressure. Just something of ourselves that grounds us in Beauty's harmony and freshness. Working with flowers or paints or gourmet foods or old furniture or words on a page can give us this time of creative solitude we need so desperately.

Whatever we do, we need to let it flow. We need to play with it, fiddle with it, and arrange it until the cake says, "I'm done," or the story says, "The end," or the canvas gives us a broad smile with no missing teeth.

It is our nature to create something. We are not just creations of God; we are cocreators with a divine Artist who continues to arrange for us new possibilities out of the colors and textures of our lives. When we offer our creative efforts to God, we are gathering up all the scatterings of our days and arranging them into something that makes sense to us.

Something of our own.

It is like offering to God and the world a bouquet of flowers that we've hidden behind our backs, something fresh that we grew and tended ourselves. What joy we bring to Beauty's face!

I have an artist friend, Jean, who also works part-time as a paleontologist's assistant on construction sites in downtown Los Angeles. When she isn't looking for fossils, she gathers raw clay for her sculptures. Sometimes she even sculpts on the work site and creates truly amazing prehistoric creatures, using bits of caliche for the eyes and teeth. She sculpts these little art pieces amid the machinery and dust and hard hats. It is as if these creatures were there in the earth all along, waiting to be uncovered by Jean's creative hands. And in that huge pit of caliche and clay—overlaid with deafening noises, dust, and heat—these newly formed creatures add joy to the universe.

Gathering up whatever we happen to have—and creating out of it—is an important ritual for our days, whether it be gathering raw clay or daffodils or sugar and flour.

Once a week I go alone to the beach for a couple of hours to be still, observe, pray, and write. It is my "Beauty break," during which I combine both the nurture of contemplative silence and the creativity of writing. That's how I gather up the pieces of myself and put myself back together. I have a blue-and-white–striped beach chair, a rather droopy straw hat, a notebook, a pen, and a bottle of water. That's all I need. I'm making music. I'm arranging wildflowers. I'm painting the sea. I'm more alive than ever! I am part of the creative urge within all people, an urge that Alfred North Whitehead calls the "creative advance of the world."

We are part of this wondrous creativity that lies at the heart of the universe, a "numinous energy," as cosmologist Brian Swimme says, that embraces all the chaotic elements swirling through time and fashions something utterly new—novel possibilities as fresh as sunflowers and as wild as saber-toothed tigers with caliche eyes.

In this world that appears to be falling apart at the seams, we must join this Creative Advance and regather ourselves. And in that regathering, remake the universe.

Create something. Anything. Just do it with love and a little madness.

Carve out time to play with the universe.

In the beginning…God created…
    GENESIS 1:1

Sailboats, Cookies, and Huge Philosophical Questions

God is like water, flowing throughout the universe,
like an ocean touching innumerable shores.
                    MARJORIE HEWITT SUCHOCKI

I wonder if I make a difference. Truly, unless I win the Nobel prize for peace or find a cure for AIDS or write the great American novel, will my presence here mean anything at all?

I feel helpless and inadequate in the scheme of things.

I ponder this on my way down to the beach. In my bag, along with plenty of chocolate chip cookies, is a new book by Marjorie Hewitt Suchocki. *In God's Presence* is about God and water and prayer.

As I take a deep breath of salty freshness, I read:

> God's presence, like water, pervades the nooks and crannies of existence—what is the boundary of water?...Why can't the higher life form that is God also co-occupy us, flowing through and around and in us, even while remaining God, and while we remain ourselves? What if such a God affects us at the deepest levels of our being—our most subconscious psyches—as well as at our "edges" in our interaction with the rest of the world?[1]

I look up at the swooping cranes and the waves crashing against rock. The rolling breakers release into a flat, smooth silkiness that glides onto shore in a kind of oceanic sigh. I take out a cookie and taste it with great satisfaction. These are the nooks and crannies. All this—from the ineffable elegance of water and cranes to the chewy cookie melting into my childhood memories of my mother's kitchen—God feels and knows and loves and cherishes.

It all matters.

Perhaps life is not "an empty bubble on the sea of nothingness," as Jean-Paul Sartre would say and as I sometimes feel. Perhaps, instead, life is cocreation. And in that mix of wind and sunburned feet and messy cookies, something meaningful and lasting is happening after all.

"God works with the world as it is in order to bring it to where it can be," says Marjorie. So when we pray, "prayer changes the way the world is, and therefore changes what the world can be. Prayer opens the world to its own transformation."

Changing the world with prayer? Really? Ah! My days of existential angst are numbered. Hope is settling in.

---

[1]Marjorie Hewitt Suchocki, *In God's Presence: Theological Reflections on Prayer* (St. Louis: Chalice Press, 1996), 9.

The scent of the sea suddenly lures me out of my book. I see a little sailboat swimming gracefully on the surface of diamonds, harnessing the wind and working with it to move where it chooses. It is as if the wind and the boat are partners in a contrapuntal dance.

Our prayers must be like the sailboat, working together with a greater power to find a meaningful path through the vast sea. Prayer, then, is a kind of partnership with the Wind.

As the sailboat slides off out of sight and the seagulls swoop down unendingly for food, it all seems to be a dance of deeply interconnected joy! Marjorie writes, "Prayer is God's invitation to us to be willing partners in the great dance of bringing a world into being that reflects something of God's character." Our basis for prayer, then, is this "great communion" with God.

So today I am reminded that prayer does make a difference to the world. I make a difference! Sitting here on this day in my seemingly useless beach-bumming bliss, I am changing the world.

And when I pray...

When I pray, angels are swooping like gulls into the heart of God's endless caress of everything. My prayers are gifts to the universe.

Praying with the seagulls! Praying with the wind! My prayer for the people in the Middle East gives God this new thing to work with that wasn't in the world before. A small dent in the scheme of things, but still it is something.

Something God cherishes.

It is time to put on my shoes, pack up my things, and go home to reflect on this day, on the gems I have collected in my mind and heart from this place and this book. I leave reluctantly, but with a new sense of Beauty as empowerment to make a difference in this gorgeous, tragic world of mine.

And after he had dismissed the crowds, he went up the mountain by himself to pray.
MATTHEW 14:23

24

A Tree in Winter

Through the empty branches the sky remains.
It is what you have.

RAINER MARIA RILKE

Cincinnati, Ohio. 1994. Following the death of my father.

The pear tree outside my kitchen window is gray and stark below the wintry sky of January. It unsettles me in its stillness, its austerity—its dark, eerie shadows looming over everything. Just a few months ago my pear tree was full of color, thick with lush, reddish leaves, and hesitant to give up its colorful cloak until the very last possible moment.

It saddened me at first, knowing that the tree would be naked and cold for several months. But today I find myself gazing with new eyes at the barren limbs as they stand in relief against the snow-heavy sky.

In an instant my sentiment about the tree changes from sadness to wonder. Because, you see, the tree has taken on a new dignity, a strength that I could not know when it was covered over with thick, soft leaves. Now there is a contemplative air about the tree in contrast to the constant stirring of leaves as they grow, change, dance in the summer breeze, die, and fall. It is as if the tree, which gave up all its fruit and color, now is cloaked in a simple, elegant beauty, its brownish twisting branches reaching longingly toward the huge, vast, white sky.

In our own lives, we go through seasons in which we feel that all the fruit and sweetness has dropped away, spoiled, and decayed. We feel naked and vulnerable. Lost. Disillusioned.

Perhaps we feel abandoned by another person, feel that we have utterly failed, or feel purposeless in a sea of mindless activity. Or we may simply be in the midst of personal grief, a tragic loss, a season when all we have is the sky.

These are the times we can become like the tree—strong and full of grace—as we allow ourselves to be still and reflect on our lives.

We can be sure that our suffering is not forever. Winter will give way to spring. The sap will rise again to nourish new life. But in the interim—while we are suffering or empty or grieving—we can gain courage by knowing that our very stillness and starkness can be our strength.

We can thrive in our new vision of the open sky that was lost to us before. There are things we were blind to in summer. Now, the sky is all we have, as Rilke says.

And that is enough for now.

With loss or suffering, we recognize how fast circumstances can change. We long for some kind of sturdiness and life in the roots of the tree. We look deep inside ourselves to find these divine roots in the midst of winter's storms and barrenness. In the stillness of winter, we find patience to bear the pain, to live through it, to survive. We cry out in hope with Percy Bysshe Shelley, " O, Wind, if Winter comes, can Spring be far behind?"

During our days of spiritual winter, we can search for our roots again, the source of our deepest yearnings. That source is Beauty, proud and tall, rugged and full of fruit not seen. The root of our being, our beautiful God, feels the barren cold in our paralyzed limbs and promises us eternal spring.

We need to find our way down into these divine, compassionate roots, and with this steadiness reach upward, stretching, holding our own as gracefully as we can while our vision expands to new worlds of understanding and feeling.

We can—if we are still and quiet like the tree—find a steady, contemplative flow of life, perhaps in a time of daily meditation, prayer, and spiritual reflection.

You may want to find a tree to study, draw, or touch. You may just want to listen to it or speak to it. Trees have a song; they own a particular music that many people do not know of.

Listen to them.

"I said to the almond tree," says Nikos Kazantzakis, "'Sister, speak to me of God,' And the almond tree blossomed."

Spring will come again if we do not deny our winters. And when it does, our roots will be more firmly planted because we have survived another winter, another loss, another heartbreak. And out of our loss comes a new moment of creativity and growth. A new bud appears.

We know that we are planted in the divine flow of life and that, come what may, we will survive. So let us embrace our loss and discover an Eternal Blooming.

> *They are like trees*
> *planted by streams of water,*
> *which yield their fruit in its season.*
> PSALM 1:3

Kissing the Earth with Our Feet

People say that walking on water is a miracle, but to me, walking peacefully on the Earth is the real miracle.

THICH NHAT HANH

The virginal sunlight graces the morning as timid yellow flowers hold themselves shut, waiting to unfold. As I walk along this familiar path in the park, I feel as though the dew of the unsoiled day has washed everything clean, including picnic tables, tennis courts, trees, and me. A snow-white seagull waddles through the dewy grass, alone and perfectly content. Dogs, who always look happy, look even happier. Fellow walkers smile and greet me with extra warmth on this extravagantly beautiful morning.

This is where I begin my day, my dreams, my thoughts. Here my feelings stir inside me safely. Graceful thoughts come easily. Nothing difficult I feel or think can threaten the glory of this morning. The world is too beautiful for anything else.

It is in these moments that God's tender presence is most clear, fresh, shimmering with the zest of the day's possibilities. What is Beauty's luminous presence urging me to think...feel...do?

The tiny yellow flowers are beginning to unfold now, opening up to the irresistible charm of the sun's radiance. Unconsciously, I have been holding my arms tightly crossed, protectively, against the morning chill. The yellow flowers give me courage to unlock myself and move my arms freely, standing tall. I am open to the world now, to the infinite possibilities of the day.

27

I walk. Thoughts move in and out of my mind with no particular fuss. I just walk, alert to all around me and all within me. Sometimes I take a phrase with me to repeat, such as a line from poetry. Today it is from Rainer Maria Rilke:

"I want to unfold.

Let no place in me hold itself closed."

Sometimes I take a Taizé CD in order to sing inwardly the songs of peace, or I walk to a Bach fugue to settle my mind.

This is walking meditation, and it is a practice that brings peace and freshness and a renewed sense of joy in the world.

God knows we need it.

Quite unlike this glorious sunlit day, there is a stuffy place inside us where worries, self-doubts, cynicism, and misspoken words linger. In this place we guard so protectively, heaviness slows down our stride and makes harsh lines between our brows. What we need, I think, is a practice like walking meditation so that we might unfold in warmth, a place to let the morning dew clean out our lurking doubts, hurts, and fears–a place to find Beauty lavishly spilling over everything in sight.

Meditation, whether it be walking or sitting, is a special form of prayer that centers us, restores us–as the clean light of morning does. I like walking meditation because it embraces all the senses (and gets me out of my computer chair). But this is not "power walking," which only makes me think that life is one big hurried rat race. That is for another time. This is a walk of peace.

Thich Nhat Hanh, Buddhist monk and Nobel Peace Prize nominee, is quite famous for his walking meditation practice. Many people from around the world have walked in silence with him, enjoying each step, each breath, the sky, the birds, the fragrances of a world that sorely needs to be loved and embraced.

Thich Nhat Hanh teaches us to walk in beauty, accepting all, letting go of all. There is never a need to force things out of one's mind, but rather let Beauty herself be the wind for us. Let us walk as the Buddhists walk.

Walk and touch peace every moment.
Walk and touch happiness every moment.
Each step brings a fresh breeze.
Each step makes a flower bloom.
Kiss the Earth with your feet.

Bring the Earth your love and happiness.
The earth will be safe
When we feel safe in ourselves.[1]

For you have delivered my soul from death,
    and my feet from falling,
so that I may walk before God
    in the light of life.
                    PSALM 56:13

Sleeping Beauty

Americans will not survive and flourish until all the world
survives and flourishes.

                                    BENJAMIN BARBER

Beauty is the only answer to terror. But Beauty is only skin deep
and illusory if it does not include all within its harmonies.
All.
Anything less than this is counterfeit Beauty, a thin and precarious
façade that will eventually crumble.
I think of people—such as me—who live in beautiful places with
golden opportunities and supersized grocery stores and malls that
offer free gifts of lipstick and perfume in pretty packages for a
purchase of $39.00 or more.
Half the world waits in bread lines.
I think of beautiful people in their splendid homes—people who
are much richer than I can imagine—and yet they flourish at the
expense of the rest of the world.
We, the blessed ones, are for the most part asleep.
When will we wake up to this significant reality of our
interdependence with the rest of the world? When will history's
bloody repetition dawn on us, that the oppressed will rise up against
the oppressors?
And when will we face the painful truth that we are—in the whole

---

[1]Thich Nhat Hanh: *The Long Road Turns to Joy: A Guide to Walking Meditation* (Berkeley,
Calif.: Parallax Press, 1996), 67.

scheme of things—oppressors? When will we understand that we need to include all at the table of plenty, or we will all perish?

Do we want to wake up?

The path away from terror and toward Beauty lies here—in our ability to wake up to our responsibility to the whole. To include all contrasts of viewpoint, color, and style into the mix. To share what we have with others. "To live simply so that others may simply live." To work passionately for justice outside our borders as well as within. To envision education and jobs and health care for all people of the world—no matter how different or strange these people appear to us—as if they were our brothers and sisters. Which they are. But will we dare to look beyond ourselves?

Beauty sleeps.

This sleep is further drugged by violence and war and demonization of the "other" while the root causes of terror—ignorance and poverty and exclusion—are blasted into oblivion.

Beauty in full bloom knows no boundaries of concern. All contrasts and seemingly incompatible colors can be woven creatively together in patterns of justice and well-being for the whole.

Beauty is sleeping in my beloved America.

Where, oh where, is our prince?

Awake, O harp and lyre!
I will awake the dawn.
I will give thanks to you, O Lord, among the peoples;
I will sing praises to you among the nations.
For your steadfast love is as high as the heavens;
your faithfulness extends to the clouds.
PSALM 57:8–10

PART 2

Embracing Beauty in Adventure and Misadventure

The Adventure of the Universe starts with a dream and reaps tragic Beauty.

ALFRED NORTH WHITEHEAD,
ADVENTURES OF IDEAS

Just over the Ridge

[Love] does not look to the future; for it finds its own reward in the immediate present.

ALFRED NORTH WHITEHEAD

Sometimes happiness seems to be just ahead of us, just over the ridge, just beyond the next curve. We're almost there…yes…we're almost there…almost!

This is one of the greatest fibs of human experience.

I vividly remember hiking up a mountain near Taos, New Mexico, with my husband, Ron. It was our honeymoon. The bright, blue New Mexico sky invited us upward to the rocky mountain bathed in light and shadow, dotted with pine and ash trees. The crisp morning air promised us a comfortable adventure.

But by noon the Southwestern sun was getting pretty hot.

I was young and healthy, but being more of a bookworm than an athlete, I complained most of the way up. Ron, good-hearted and optimistic—and in much better shape than I—went on ahead, forging our path with the rigorous spirit of a true mountain man.

Constantly suggesting that we stop at this rock or under that tree and take a break, I was always lagging behind. Ron would cajole me into moving forward by saying, "The top is just over there!" When we got to that spot he had pointed out, I realized it was not the top. Undaunted, Ron would again exclaim, "The top is just over there!" and point to another ridge that was supposed to be the top. But inevitably when we got there, it was not the top. This went on for a couple of hours before I finally caught on to this exasperating game conspired between the mountain and my husband.

I don't think we ever really made it to the top. I can't remember the details, but I probably feigned illness or faked an injury in order to get us going back downhill. But I do remember quite dramatically the "always wanting to be there but never quite being there" feeling.

Never quite being there is actually where we are most of the time. We can be miserable in the midst of it, complaining all the way. Or we can be right where we are, enjoy the scenery along the way, and not worry so much about the top. Now that I'm older and wiser (I avoid mountain hikes altogether unless there is a Starbucks on the way up), I realize that much of my life was spent with this belief. I'll be happy once I get married...I'll be happy once I graduate from college...I'll be happy once I get the right job...I'll be happy when I have that antique lamp...Happiness was always just over the ridge, but never there.

The journey up—regardless of how far we actually go—can be exhilarating if we quit focusing on the elusive top and enjoy the budding moments in the now. The mixed bag of "now" with all its sweet nothings—stopped-up sinks, freeway backups, hilarity, soft breezes, and backaches—is actually a very nice place to be. Why? The present is where our source of happiness is: It's where God is! God is certainly envisioning the mountaintop with us, but God is actually right where we are in the hot noonday sun, feeling the cool breeze and burning blisters alike.

Having goals infuses life with energy, meaning, and imagination. But fixating on goals at the expense of life in the now cheapens our goals and deceives us into thinking that happiness is just over the ridge.

We Americans are intoxicated with five-year plans, but we stumble clumsily over the here and now, as Dick Van Dyke did with his ottoman. If we don't balance that desirable future vision with a sweet embrace of the present landscape, the goal will mean nothing once we get there.

After September 11, many of us have decided that life needs to be lived in all its intensity of feeling. Right now. That is Beauty's call to transformation, feeling deeply in the here and now. It is a good thing.

As you read this, Beauty is exploding around you. Birds are singing; worms are inching across your front porch; cats are sharpening their claws (on your good furniture); and people are falling in love. There is so much to see, feel, touch, and celebrate! Be mindful. Be alert.

There is so much Beauty just aching to be embraced.

And contrary to Ron's stalwart "onward and upward" mind-set, even he now realizes that taking rests along the way is a good thing.

The here and now is chock full of eye-popping vistas, cool streams, and romantic walks. Don't miss them.

Embrace the journey.

"Look at the birds of the air; they neither sow nor reap nor gather into barns, and yet your heavenly Father feeds them. Are you not of more value than they?"
MATTHEW 6:26

A Thousand Cranes

Prayer is naught else but a yearning of the soul...
when it is practiced with the whole heart, it has great power.

MECHTHILD OF MAGDEBURG

Eating Japanese food for the first time felt like my first time in a swimming pool. I was all at once excited, terrified, and thankful someone experienced was there to keep me from drowning. Our friends from Tokyo, Mitsue and Takao, took my husband and me to an authentic Japanese restaurant in Los Angeles. They promised to help us wade into this adventure slowly.

They began with familiar things such as tuna and chicken and then slipped in the raw fish before we knew what was happening. The sushi went down without incident. But the salmon eggs were another matter. Oh, I could do very well without the sound—and taste—of salmon eggs popping in my mouth!

While Mitsue ordered the green tea ice cream for everyone, I asked Takao about the name of the restaurant, "A Thousand Cranes." He explained to me that this name is very significant in Japanese tradition. Making paper cranes is an ancient origami art that Japanese children learn early on. The tradition says that if you fold one thousand paper cranes, your prayers will have more power.

Takao explained that in the cancer wards in Japanese hospitals there are origami cranes hanging over the beds of many of the patients (one thousand per patient, of course). The families and friends of the sick diligently fold beautiful paper—and fold and fold—a thousand times. Takao and Mitsue made some paper cranes out of their napkins, right there at table, to show us how it is done.

As I studied these tiny, artful birds, I thought of all the caring family members and friends of the sick who lovingly work deep into the night, with tired hands, folding each delicate scrap of paper into a lovely, tiny crane. It reminds me of the thousands of candles lit across the United States on the Friday night after the September 11 tragedy. There is something very powerful in making our prayers not only visible, but numerous like the stars.

A thousand cranes, a thousand candles, a thousand prayers! The more numerous the stars, the more beautiful the sky!

You've heard the phrase "Less is more." That may work for purple eye shadow and salmon eggs, but in the case of prayer, more is always better. The reason more is better is because God hears and feels our prayers, every one, and works with them to bring about something beautiful in the world.

God truly needs our prayers! If God worked out the details of life regardless of what we pray, then prayers would be useless. It would be silly to waste our time lighting candles or making paper cranes.

But God does not work in a vacuum, determining alone how things unfold in the world. It's simply not the way the universe works. In this relational cosmos, God works *with* the world, with our prayers, with our paper cranes, with our candles.

Our prayers add to the richness of Beauty's work in the world. A thousand cranes are better than one or even 999! The more prayers, the more Beauty we thrust into the heart of the universe, breaking down walls of hate and ignorance by the sheer enormity of blessings pouring into the world.

That's why prayer is an adventure, like eating Japanese food or learning to swim. While you are praying, you don't know what's up ahead. You just know that the future is not set in stone, that you have some part in shaping it.

Prayer is a power you hold in your hand.

A lot of loving people are willing to help us wade through the adventure together. Like cranes flying in formation across the grand blue sky, we fly together with God into the future made artfully out of prayers.

I will probably not eat sushi or salmon eggs anytime soon. For me, one salmon egg is enough for a lifetime. But prayer is a whole other matter. When I think I've prayed enough, I will look up at the stars and think of those paper cranes in Japanese cancer wards, and I will pray some more.

I will not forget that in this world of ethnic cleansing, greed, terrorism, ignorance, and poverty, God needs our prayers. It doesn't matter how we do it–through meditation, corporate prayer, written prayers, affirmations, visualization, prayers made out of poetic feelings or put on canvas, prayers put into song or sounds of silence, prayers folded into little birds–when we pray in any of these ways and a thousand more, we are making a difference.

Like a thousand fluttering paper cranes cheering on a sick child, prayers add something to Beauty's richness and power in the world.

Pray without ceasing.
1 THESSALONIANS 5:17

Breathing Easy

The morning wind spreads its fresh smell.
We must get up and take that in,
That wind that lets us live.
Breathe before it's gone.

RUMI

It's the wee hours of the morning.

I'm waking up, dreaming that I'm being smothered with a fat feather pillow. But dreaming is too close to reality. I am suffocating from an asthma attack. I had gone to bed exhausted but tranquil after a trip to San Francisco. I had just arrived home, splashed water on my face, put my head on the soft familiar pillow, and fallen into a sweet sleep with dreams of San Francisco's Ghirardelli Chocolate Drops dancing above my head.

Now it's 3:00 a.m., and I can't breathe. I'm drowning in an ocean and can't get to the surface. I'm going die. I'm going to die. I just know it!

(Well, at least I got to see San Francisco.)

I'm at a loss. My husband is at a loss. The cats are at a loss. We all bolt up in bed and do the only thing we know how to do: panic.

36

Finally, my husband—the smart one—has the wits to know that I need to get to the hospital and onto oxygen. And I did.

This feeling of suffocation is not just physical. When New York and Washington were attacked, my first response to the news was strangled breath. It was hours after the initial shock before I could breathe normally. Is it any wonder that we have trouble breathing? When it seems the world is going to hell in a handbasket, breathing gets strangled. We are swept into the deep waters of disbelief, insecurity, and terror as if there is not enough air in the world to sustain us. How many times do you lie awake at night—in the wee hours, when the dragons of dread attack—and feel as though you're drowning in an ocean of fear?

Breathing isn't as easy as we think.

But the good news is that there is plenty of air after all. There is a breath—a lavishly generous, full, and spacious breath—in the universe that will keep us afloat. Her name is Beauty.

To get a sense of this Breath, imagine a warm, radiant light flowing into you, filling every nook and cranny of your being. This light-filled energy connects you to everything in the world and then rests gently inside you, filling you with freshness, warmth, and tranquility, even when everything outside is out of your control.

This is God's breath. This is divine Beauty, who feels everything as she breathes in and transforms everything as she breathes out. One breath at a time.

Like the rhythm of an ocean tide, God's breathing takes in our starkest feelings and breathes out a new thing. Nothing goes unfelt. It just gets breathed into something beautiful.

Your breath is beautiful. Your breath is original. Your breath offers something new into the universe. Each breath grounds you in Beauty's creative, transforming presence. Your job is simply to breathe with Beauty in her oceanic rhythm and her calming wisdom.

When we panic, we need to do two things. First, we need to use our wits to take care of the immediate problem if there is anything to be done. Or if we are without wits, we need to find someone around who has them.

Second, we need to feel our own breath and let all else go. If you have trouble with this, study a cat; notice not only its ability to sleep eighteen hours a day but also its calming purr that speaks of another world where overdue bills are simply sat on and clothes not put away only make soft and interesting places to sleep. We can learn to be calm in messy circumstances or in troubling emotional states when we learn to breathe with Beauty. We can, in fact, breathe in the whole world in all of its glory and horror, and then exhale with peace by breathing with the loving God who breathes alongside every ache and every tear and every loss.

Breathe in the world as it is. Then feel the intermingling of your breath with this oceanic breath of Beauty. As you breathe out, know that divine Beauty is offering something fresh, something utterly new. Let go to this fresh wind that sweeps through the universe in quiet wisps of air.

There is no reason to fear. Just breathe. Just breathe. Each breath contributes to the Spirit's tenderly transforming movements in the world. And when you finally breathe your last breath, it's OK. Beauty will keep you buoyant as your final breath flows into the vast ocean of God's heart. And that is a good place to be.

For God never stops breathing.

Then the LORD God formed man from the dust of the ground, and breathed into his nostrils the breath of life; and the man became a living being.
GENESIS 2:7

Chocolate Dreams and Pansies

Adventure rarely reaches its predetermined end.
Columbus never reached China. But he discovered America.

ALFRED NORTH WHITEHEAD

"Tea for two?" the smiling hostess in the long velvet dress asks as we walk into the front door of the McCharles Tea House. Resisting the urge to tap dance on the wooden floor to the old "Tea for Two" number, I follow her to our little table in the corner of this old Victorian cottage with my husband close behind.

It's Valentine's Day, and I'm one happy valentine. My husband has brought me here to this exquisite place of Victorian charm and beauty for a romantic tea. And here is where my valentine dreams become realized with what is called on the pretty McCharles House menu the "Chocolatea."

My wildest dreams have come true with the Chocolatea: an afternoon with nothing but chocolate—chocolate scones, chocolate-covered apricots, chocolate sandwiches, chocolate trifle, chocolate cake, and even chocolate tea! All my expectations are met and exceeded in this extremely decadent tea-time madness.

But then comes the pansy.

The waitress brings each of us a lovely, freshly picked pansy and places it next to the chocolate sandwiches. "This was grown in our garden, and it is for you to eat with your tea."

"Eat with my tea? What in the world are you talking about?" I ask.

"Just take a petal and roll it up, place it in your sandwich, and enjoy. Or you may wish simply to dip it in the cream and eat it that way."

"You're kidding, right?"

No, she's not kidding.

She looks disappointed at my barbarian response on this refined gesture, so I take one of the soft white petals from my pansy, roll it up, touch it lightly with cream, and eat it. Pleased with the sensation, I eat another, and another.

"Are you going to eat your pansy or not?" I ask my husband, eyeing the bright purple flower next to his scone.

I liked the pansy, not only because of the delicate flavor, but because of the novel experience it gave me—outside the chocolate sphere completely. It reminds me not only that there's more to life than chocolate but that the expectations we have about life and the future are often too small. We dream chocolate dreams but never imagine in a million years eating pansies!

God's eternal vision is full of novel possibilities not yet realized in the world. Even when we think we have all the angles figured out, something new pops up. That is how scientific discoveries are born, and that is how creative lives are lived. And some of these novel possibilities are unimaginable to us until they simply show up on our plates.

Did you ever imagine as a child that you would be talking to people through a computer rather than a telephone? Or that you would be doing what you're doing now, when you dreamed of being a firefighter or a ballerina? Life is not so predictable, which is unsettling on the one hand, but very exciting on the other.

Embrace Beauty by looking for novelty in each day and in each project, for something fresh and out of the ordinary. Looking into the future, keep your expectations open so that while you stuff yourself with planned-out dreams, you don't miss the pansy.

Divine Beauty is rich with variety, novelty, and pansies of every color. Let's begin to think of our spiritual journey in more lively, serendipitous ways. As my good friend and fellow writer Bruce Epperly says, envision your life as a "Holy Adventure."

Thank God today for all the unthinkable joys in your future, for serendipity, for that which we cannot even imagine in our wildest chocolate dreams.

For you are great and do wondrous things;
you alone are God.
PSALM 86:10

When the Creek Rises

God is the Great Companion—the fellow sufferer who
understands.

ALFRED NORTH WHITEHEAD

Growing up in rural Oklahoma during the 1960s and 1970s had its advantages. If your grammar was bad, nobody noticed (except for my mother). If you said "pitcher" instead of "picture," nobody cared (except for my mother).

But Oklahomans I knew had a deft saying that is much smarter than just about any saying I've ever heard. When you asked them if they were going to be somewhere, say, church on Sunday, they just might reply, "I'll be there, if the Lord is willing and the creek don't rise." I know, it's not your English class response, but it is theologically savvy. This saying suggests that there is more to our life situations than just the Lord's will. Sometimes the Lord's will is swept away tragically by the darned creek that keeps rising.

"Everything has a reason" is probably the most overused New Age cliché of the 1990s. Some people find it comforting to think that everything that happens is somehow God's will or related to God's mysterious plan. I'm not one of those people. In fact, I think such a philosophy is a bunch of baloney.

This Oklahoma girl much prefers "If the Lord is willing and the creek don't rise." This statement admits that there is more than God's will. There is God's will, yes, but there is also a huge, tragic world that God lives in with us–a world of contradictions and disappointments, a world full of atrocities that make our hair stand on end.

God's will is often thwarted by rising creeks that sweep away the good that God intends. When terrorists plan murder in the name of God, when children die in car accidents, and when whole families are wiped out in airplane crashes, God's will is certainly not being actualized. God help us if we think these are part of any "mysterious" divine plan!

Every event is made up of many influences alongside the will of God. This includes our feelings, our actions, the laws of physics, the state of our bodies, the past, and things such as hatred and greed and deep resentment seething in the heads of people living in ignorance and poverty.

God is interrelated with everything–rivers and people and chimpanzees and tiny blades of grass. There is no place that God is not. Even in suffering, God is there. Our "Great Companion" wades through the muck and along the precarious footing with us, keeping us buoyant.

We are partners with God in bringing about Beauty. Evil happens when the world chooses to go the opposite direction from Beauty's lure. All the little prejudices and hurts and resentments oftentimes build up and flood into hugely evil acts.

And it breaks the heart of God.

Beauty seems to be lost! But we know differently. Beauty cannot be drowned. It cannot be swept away. It will not give up or give in. And in the ruins of tragedy, God never stops luring, creating, transforming, redeeming, and loving things back into life and wholeness.

Our mission in this world is to be sensitive to that Beauty, which is God within us. We need to feed it and protect it fiercely–this ravishingly beautiful, divine part of us that is luring us toward the good, toward all that enhances life and well-being on this planet.

And even when catastrophic evil threatens to drown all tenderness, all rationality, all sense of justice in the world–even then, God gathers up our salty tears into a wide, wide ocean of healing love. Nothing is lost forever; all is saved in God's tender care. This is our hope. This is our comfort.

We can rest here.

So remember this bit of Oklahoma wisdom. Instead of blaming God when the creek rises, look for generosity of spirit and loving actions. Look for creative transformation. Look for kindness.

Do this, and you will be looking straight into the heart of God.

"I am with you always, to the end of the age."
MATTHEW 28:20

The Perfect Hat

God is in the details.
LUDWIG MIES VAN DER ROHE

The search for the perfect hat has taken me twenty years. I've tried them all. Straw–too hard. Cloth–too droopy. Canvas–too cowboy-looking. I've tried extra-wide–brimmed, which always catches the wind and makes me feel as if I'm the "flying nun." I once found a golf hat that stuck tightly to the head, but it left a Frankenstein-like band of red indentations across my forehead.

But then one fortuitous day I found it–*it*–the hat of my dreams, hanging so sweetly on the rack in a little out-of-the-way store. The moment I laid eyes on it, I felt it was already mine. It had to be–it was perfect in shape and color and had that certain mysterious *je ne sais quoi.*

But its proud good looks led me to believe it would be too expensive for my budget. Oh, what the heck? I'll try it on.

Ah! Perfection.

What more could I say than, "I don't care how much this costs!" But as luck would have it, the hat was a mere $17.00. Now I've spent three times that much on hats that I don't like, but this one was worth much more. And I'll tell you frankly, if I were held at gunpoint, I would say, "Take my purse, take my money, take my car, but don't lay a hand on my hat."

Recently I left my hat at the home of friends. I felt quite alone without it. These friends called me immediately when they found it and returned it promptly, as if it were a precious gem. Somehow they knew it was no ordinary hat. The hat simply isn't ordinary, even if it is inexpensive. It's made of one hundred percent vegetable fiber, which sounds like Metamucil. And I suppose if I were feeling the need, I could eat it. People do speak of eating their hats.

But no, never! This is no ordinary hat.

What makes this hat so special is that it can change shape to fit my mood or my needs. When lying in the sun, I can pull the pliable brim down to cover my face. When I'm riding in the convertible, it magically stays on in the wind! When I want to feel as if I'm Greta Garbo, I pull one side over my eyes and put on big, flashy sunglasses. The hat is for all seasons, all moods, and every single situation that involves sunshine, style, or mystery.

My hat is divine, positively divine, and I mean that seriously. My hat is one of those details in life where I find God. God is hidden in that hat—some tiny piece of the divine is nestled in vegetable fiber that bends and moves and protects me from the ravages of UV rays (or a bad hair day). I feel close to God when I wear the hat because God moves with me wherever I go, in expansive, intimate connection. In every situation, God is working with my changing needs and experiences to bring about well-being for myself and all creation.

Ah, Beauty! So perfectly matching the needs of those who wear You.

Sometimes we think of perfection as unbending, but my hat tells me otherwise. Perhaps God is perfect as my hat is perfect, not like the hard helmet of a motorcycle police officer, but a pliable, ever-creative God who works with me just where I am to bring about Beauty in each moment.

Do you feel a sense of being loved by something that fits you perfectly, no matter what is happening to you? If not, then look for your divine hat. It's waiting for you, hanging right there, in the details of your life.

> *Out of Zion, the perfection of beauty,*
> *God shines forth.*
> PSALM 50:2

When Things Fall Out

Each tree and leaf and star show how the universe is part of this one cry, that every life is noted and is cherished, and that nothing loved is ever lost or perished.

MADELEINE L'ENGLE

It could have fallen anywhere. At the produce section of the grocery store, in the busy waiting room at the dentist office, along the winding trail where I take my morning walks. It could have fallen into a drain. God forbid, it could have fallen into the toilet and been flushed into the nether world below!

But it fell onto the dark, emerald green carpet in my home right in my own bedroom, and it fell at night before bed, waiting to be found in the early morning light. My diamond—my only diamond, the one that has perched faithfully in my engagement ring for twenty-four years—fell out of its setting and onto the emerald green carpet without a sound.

Without warning. It just fell.

It could have fallen anywhere, but it chose to fall in a most auspicious place. My husband discovered it with surprise the next morning. His not-so-good vision without glasses still picked up the tiny brilliant light. The sweeper could have whooshed it away. The cats could have swallowed it. Oh, all that did *not* happen to this tiny, shiny thing that I have treasured for twenty-four years!

We could have bought another one. Yes, a bigger one. But no—this is the one I have kept close to my heart, the one we picked out together in our financially slim days of seminary when we couldn't even afford a matinee at the movies. It was small, but it was huge—hugely beautiful, signifying a commitment that would last a lifetime.

Finding the lost diamond on the emerald green carpet was a blessing of great proportion. I felt gratitude, yes. And awe. And a sense that God knows when things fall out. Precious things. Like friends that pass away or dreams that fall out of the sky. Like sunbeams that dance playfully on the sea at twilight, now gone into the cold and empty darkness. People and things and dreams fall out sometimes.

But if we look into the deep and rich hues of our faith, we will find these precious stones of our lives shimmering in a new place, waiting to be found and treasured in a new way. All is not lost. Our loved ones shimmer in a new "setting" that we call heaven. Our lost dreams dazzle more brilliantly than ever when spotted against the rich, dark mysteries of life.

God knows when things fall out or fall down or fall apart. And God knows that precious things—people we have loved or joy that doesn't sparkle as it once did—these things, like my diamond, are not lost. They have fallen onto the deep, soft places of God's heart, where they are loved and mended and made whole.

Nothing is lost in God's eternal embrace, for it can hold everything big and small. Precious things are not whooshed away. They don't get flushed. They are close by even if we can't see them, because nothing of value perishes.

Oh, the wonder of this tiny, shiny thing that was found even before it was lost! I think God's huge embrace must wrap clear around the world, scooping up diamonds like falling stars and giving them eternal brightness.

Love never ends.
1 Corinthians 13:8

The Adventure of Ideas

I put forward as a general definition of civilization, that a civilized society is exhibiting the five qualities of Truth, Beauty, Adventure, Art, Peace.

ALFRED NORTH WHITEHEAD

I've had some grand adventures in my life. I've walked through the favelas of Brazil, sat in the shadow of the Parthenon, and stepped behind the "Iron Curtain" (which says something about my age). I've shaken hands with the President of the United States, and I've been to Disneyland. What more could a person ask for?

Much more.

The adventures that I have felt to be most compelling in my life are not physical adventures at all, but the adventures of *ideas*. Whether it is reading new findings about the origin of the universe or a fresh interpretation of a familiar biblical text, ideas can take us to new places, even if we don't have the money or energy to go to Singapore.

I find that ideas can take me mountaineering through peak after peak of "aha!" experiences. But most often, it's not just *reading* about ideas, but *talking* about ideas with others that leads to these peak experiences. And with such interaction we find ourselves enjoying further adventures of mutual enrichment, friendship, and a sense of camaraderie. Together we seek to make meaning and solve problems not only for the sake of our individual lives but for the common good of all.

Adventure is what we are made for: plunging into new territories, daring to open up to Beauty's rich intelligence and fascinating insights. But if we are made for this, why is it so hard for us? We are often afraid to go beyond our familiar structures of thinking, like members of the Flat Earth Society who fear that they might fall off the earth if they trusted that it were round.

Sometimes we are afraid to explore the practices of other cultures or religions because we consider them a threat to our own neatly tied worldview. But if we don't attempt to expand ourselves—to be more well-rounded like the earth itself—we end up on a very flat and lifeless plain, on a planet that reluctantly hosts wars of ignorance, prejudice, terror, and fear.

Much of my graduate study in philosophy centered on philosopher Alfred North Whitehead because he took me on so many wild adventures in thinking about the world and about my place in it. In fact, he has a book entitled *Adventures of Ideas* in which he offers the reader incredible journeys through gorgeous landscapes of "Truth, Beauty, Adventure, Art, and Peace."

You can find your own adventure today by picking up a newspaper, book, or magazine article that compels you to think more deeply and imaginatively. Find a subject you want to explore and delve into it. Talk about your ideas with someone you know, someone who will appreciate your findings.

If you can't think of a single soul who would be interested, then look around for some new friends. We need fellow travelers for this journey into the adventure of ideas.

We have nothing to fear in our quest for knowledge and understanding. We will not fall off the face of the earth if we discover that it is, indeed, round.

If you indeed cry out for insight, and raise your voice for understanding; if you seek it like silver, and search for it as for hidden treasures—then you will understand the fear of the LORD and find the knowledge of God.
PROVERBS 2:3–5

47

PART 3

Embracing Beauty in Ordinary and Extraordinary People

Beauty captivates the flesh in order to obtain permission to pass right through to the soul...When the feeling for beauty happens to be associated with the sight of some human being, the transference of love is made possible, at any rate in an illusory manner. But it is all the beauty of the world, it is universal beauty, for which we yearn.

SIMONE WEIL,
GRAVITY AND GRACE

Letting It Rip

He whose body is chained, and his soul unbound, is free.

EPICTETUS

I've never been much for picnics.

It's a sweltering July day in the Santa Monica Mountains. Ants, flies, 100-degree weather—everything you need. But I am with very good friends, so who cares about the dangerous wasps clinging to my pasta salad? Yes, sitting here on a blanket overlooking the smoggy valley from whence the original valley girls were born and raised on two or three vocabulary words, I suppose you could say it was...like...*totally* cool.

The ravaging heat, annoying pests, the view of nothing much but haze—all this by itself is delightful enough. But a particular event occurs at this picnic that cuts through the haze like a razor-sharp knife.

It is a man in a wheelchair. He's a slightly balding, middle-aged man with thick glasses and strong, muscular arms. A younger man with longish hair pushes him in a sturdy, steel chair. They don't see us, but we can see them through the trees. I think nothing much of their presence in the park and go back to shooing insects and thinking small thoughts.

But then I notice that the man is being wheeled—with enormous strain on the part of the companion—to the top of a steep, rocky overlook. This rugged area is not exactly "handicap accessible." Will the chair make it? Dear God, will it turn over or fall down the mountain?

I hold my breath.

Fearless, the man and his undaunted companion push on to the very top, while I dare not blink. I watch because I can't help it. I'm frozen in fascination and fear for the man. We all watch. The man is shouting out to go onward and upward, arms waving and gesturing forward with a mad impatience.

When they finally reach the top of the overlook and stop (and I start to breathe again), the man in the chair thrusts his muscular arms high into the wind and lets out a primal scream, long and loud and wild. It echoes through the valley below, where totally cool girls shop for makeup and pretty hairpins. It cuts through the hazy view of nothing much, clear through to every small bird's nest and snake den on the mountainside. It is the sound of a man at the top of the world.

It is not the sound of a person trapped in a wheelchair. It is the sound of liberation, a divine cry that comes from somewhere deep and boundless.

I feel his wild, searing scream cut through me, right into the center of my soul, a soul that was moments ago overlaid with worries of pesky wasps. I want to feel what he is feeling, to know whatever it is that is flooding out of him, gushing madly like a torrent of pure water in a stale, dry valley. Do the girls swinging tiny, expensive handbags in the valley have any idea that a man is at this moment sitting atop a mountain above them, screaming into the wind? They go about their business, worried about tiny troubles while their souls are missing all this bigness—the sound of pure, divine, boundless exuberance!

The oppressive heat and pesky wasps take a backseat in my mind now. Something significant is happening right in front of me. I know God is speaking to me in this momentary cry of a man who knows no bounds. I feel at this moment an inkling of his freedom, his spontaneous cry into the wind of vastness. Un–self-consciously.

Layers of hazy, lazy, itsy bitsy concerns have covered up the primal scream of life. It happens. It happens to valley girls and dentists and ballerinas and teachers and ministers and mothers and me. We feel something wanting to be let out. A sound. A scream. A Divine Overcoming of all that is hard and fearful and ugly inside us and around us.

The screaming man offers me a way to cut through the fog of smallness into the vast overlook of huge vistas that take my breath away. I must take the difficult path and refuse to live in the narrow box of my infirmities. I have to dare to move against all odds to the top of the world.

And let out a howl.

When we do this, when we really let it rip, we join in Beauty's surging energy of Divine Overcoming. We are living at the center of who we really are, without back injury, without prejudice, without fear, and without pain. We are living in the Spirit of pure, boundless grace, a grace that refuses to give up or give in.

I learned on that day of wasps and heat and smog the definition of exuberance. I learned how to let go to this huge, wild, boundless Energy.

I learned what the Spirit of God sounds like.

In all these things we are more than conquerors through him who loved us.

ROMANS 8:37

Riding on a Beam of Light

My secret is I remained a child. I always asked the simplest questions. I ask them still.

ALBERT EINSTEIN

What would it be like to ride on a beam of light? A whimsical, poetic, childlike question, I thought, when I first heard it. But the fact is that the question came from the mind of sixteen-year-old Albert Einstein. And it was more than just a lovely thought. It was Einstein's *passion* to answer this question. Ten years later, in 1905, he answered it, and his answer is called the theory of relativity.

I am no physicist, but Einstein the person is a fascination to me, kind of like Mozart or Joan of Arc or van Gogh or Susan B. Anthony. Such unique individuals enter the world, struggle against the tide, follow their own light at any cost, irritate a lot of people, and leave behind world-altering accomplishments.

Back to the question. What is the answer, really? What would happen if you could ride a beam of light? Nothing, according to Einstein. Length shrinks to zero, and time stands still. Why? His answer came from the inspired notion that time itself is relative. The faster you move, the slower the time. By showing in his many "thought experiments" that time is relative, Einstein changed the way we see the world.

Einstein made this discovery in an intellectual climate that believed beyond doubt that time was absolute, unchanging. Everyone but Einstein believed that time was a perfect, unchanging tick-tock heartbeat of the universe. But Einstein would not give in to the pressure of the mainstream. He said of himself, "If I have one gift, it is that I am as stubborn as a mule."

Children are a lot like that, I believe. We think of their stubbornness as a shortcoming, something they need to grow out of, and quickly. But now we are met with a childlike man with plaintive eyes and unkempt hair who changes the world with his stubborn genius. He bucks the system, infuriates his physics professors, hangs out in cafés instead of attending classes at the university, and finally ends up as a government clerk, working six days a week, doing physics on the side.

Ah! Who would have thought that a twenty-six-year-old patent clerk who worked on physics in his spare time would alter the way we see the universe?

Maybe to "follow your bliss"—as Joseph Campbell suggests—is the philosophy we need to instill in our children and to follow ourselves. And while we're at it, we ought to take another look at stubbornness.

I can't help but think of Jesus, too, of how he came into the world, a radical nonconformist who hung out with the wrong crowd, infuriated a lot of people, and was poor to boot. But he left behind a childlike philosophy of love and forgiveness. Stubborn was his middle name. His unwillingness to compromise his values and mission led to his death, but he lives on in us. And if he does, then we are to be like him. We are to be childlike, stubborn, following our bliss, our mission, our passion.

Even if it's unpopular.

We might just change history. But if we don't, we at least change our world in subtle ways. In our stubbornness and in our passion we give to God something fresh to work with, something slightly new, off the beaten path, or even outrageously novel. But something that fires the universe into a beautiful ongoing adventure—a Divine lure that we ride like a beam of light straight into the heart of Beauty's mystery.

When the days drew near for him to be taken up, he set his face to go to Jerusalem.
    LUKE 9:51

The Gentle Weaver

She who reconciles the ill-matched threads of her life, and
weaves them gratefully into a single cloth—

RAINER MARIA RILKE

As I grow older, and hopefully wiser, I find myself observing people with great interest. Everyone is fascinating, for better or worse.

"I'm going to live in Santa Fe!" she exclaims. "I want to learn to weave a rug."

This is the most interesting person I've talked to in awhile. This is my sister.

Perhaps what makes Lexy so interesting and irresistible is not the fact that she is my own flesh and blood, but the fact that she launches her unquenchable spirit of adventure out into the world, even after being diagnosed with multiple sclerosis. Most of us would buckle under the devastating news and retreat into our room of tears and self-pity. Not Lexy. Her indomitable spirit apparently stands in a space all its own, apart from her circumstances. Not being able even to walk at times, she smiles through her voice on the telephone, undaunted with ideas of her new home in Santa Fe, a place of her dreams and longings.

She wants to weave a rug.

This, my accomplished, brilliant sister who made her mark in the medical profession, now wants nothing more but to play as a child in Santa Fe's healing sun. Her spirit seems to float above her body in a beauty that captivates my own spirit. Lexy knows the limits of her body and has no grandiose expectations of miraculous healing. She accepts what is, but will not be a victim to it. If she lives twenty years, ten years, or less, she is going to weave that rug.

What would you do if you found that you had a devastating disease?

Perhaps you would close yourself off and block out the sun for having the audacity to shine, muting all the colors into a dull gray. Or perhaps, like Lexy, you would take all the colored threads you have before you—good, bad, and in-between—and learn the art of weaving.

You could blame God for this horrible curse, making God into some kind of monster who does wicked things such as this. Or you could let go of those worn-out images of the Divine and help God weave something splendidly novel out of your life as it is. For God is the Gentle Weaver who works with each ill-matched thread to bring about novel patterns of meaning and hope. This is the God who, as Marjorie Suchocki says, "works with what is to bring about what can be." This is divine Beauty who suffers with us and brings healing of spirit when there is yet no cure for the body.

Our beautiful God brings together the many strands of our lives, even the colors that are sometimes horribly incongruous, and makes them work. This is the God who does not punish us with infirmity, but who groans with us in the darkness until that divine cry breaks open a way that only God's eternal vision can fathom.

We weave a rug. It is our gift to God, and it is beautiful beyond our imagining.

All things work together for good for those who love God.
ROMANS 8:28

Wearing Your Heart

Do not save your loving speeches
For your friends till they are dead;
Do not write them on their tombstones,
Speak them rather now instead.

ANNA CUMMINS

"Don't wear your heart on your sleeve." That saying used to torment me. Oh the shame of having people see your heart hanging there on your sleeve! I take images much too literally. Why can't it plainly say, "Don't let people see how much you care"? But that is even worse than a pumping red heart hanging off your sleeve. Both sayings lead one to becoming a person I would not much like to meet.

One Saturday morning I did a wild and silly thing. I had a heart painted on my fingernail. I was persuaded by the manicurist, who is always looking for ways to add to the bill.

"Heart on finger?"

"No thank you. That would be silly for a woman my age."

She sighs.

"Well…can you put one of those shiny 'diamonds' in the middle of the heart?"

Perhaps not becoming to a professional, this bit of silliness delighted me to no end. I felt as if I were thirteen again, and wanted to show everybody my heart on my finger, with the shiny pretend "diamond" in the center. Pure silliness! An affectation not becoming to a teacher or minister or anyone older than fifteen. But sometimes it's nice to throw conventional ideas out the window. Perhaps we need a bit of silliness every now and then. But more importantly, I like the symbolism.

Why not show off our hearts?

I mean, why not express what we feel when what we feel is love or gratitude or some other graceful feeling that adds Beauty to the world? Wearing your heart on your sleeve or your finger can be a wild and wonderful experiment, even if the world frowns on it. Try blurting out, "I like you. I love you. I appreciate you. I adore you. I miss you. I think you're pretty wonderful."

We may not have that love returned. That's a chance we'll have to take.

Remember the story in the Bible about the extraordinary woman who washed Jesus' feet with her tears? Good heavens! It was shocking! Embarrassingly so.

But her spectacle of love did not stop there. She poured expensive perfume all over his feet, kissed them over and over, and dried them with her hair. Now that was an extravagant, outrageous expression of feeling.

And what did Jesus think about all this emotional nonsense? He *loved* it! He plainly told her goody-two-shoes critics, "She has shown great love."

What's so good about keeping our hearts safely, silently, invisibly boarded up within us? We seem to have no problem wearing other emotions on our sleeves—anger, sadness, gladness. Oh, those are easy and safe. But to express openly feelings of love—that's risky. We could be rejected or misunderstood.

But if Jesus is a true expression of the Divine, we see that vulnerability and love and being rejected at times pretty much sums up the way God's costly expressions of love work in the world.

The heart on my finger is an affectation, yes, but I'm convinced that it is not an altogether silly one. I hope I never grow too old to wear my heart on my finger.

> *Then turning toward the woman, he said to Simon, "Do you see this woman? I entered your house; you gave me no water for my feet, but she has bathed my feet with her tears and dried them with her hair."*
> LUKE 7:44

The Glee Club

We find a delight in the beauty and happiness of children that makes the heart too big for the body.
RALPH WALDO EMERSON

His eyes were bright. That's what I remember the most. The little boy who changed my day had bright, clear eyes. He ran up to me on the beach and held out his hand while his eyes shined.

"Do you see it?" he shouted.

"See what?" I asked.

"The sand crab!" he squealed.

Then I saw a tiny movement in the palm of his sandy hand.

"Ah, yes!"

"I just put my hand in the sand and when I pulled it out I was holding it!"

"How wonderful!"

Then he ran away, half leaping, half skipping, looking for another lucky person to share his joy. I don't know that little boy, but he made me want to join the "glee club." Thinking about his smiling eyes and skinny little legs running up to show me the sand crab, I wonder if any better word can describe that moment.

"Glee," according to Webster, is defined as "merriment, mirth; gaiety; exhilaration." What are these but Beauty's gifts?

Children have it. They know what glee means.

What happens to us as we get older? What mutes the exhilaration of the little miracles and joys of life? When was the last time you leaped or skipped or squealed about anything?

This little boy has so much to teach me about God, about Beauty's sphere, about what life is like before we grow old and cynical and subdued. The excitement of one tiny sand crab was enough to catapult this little boy into a world where everything is pure grace. This is a world where sand crabs come out to entertain, where people stop what they are doing to share in the joy, and where we can't seem to jump high enough to capture the joy of the moment.

This glee club only accepts members who believe in such a world, a world that sings "All things bright and beautiful, the Lord God made them all." Ah, yes, this is the God of glee! Believing in the God of glee instead of a God of gloom may be our first step in the initiation process.

Look around you this week. Is there something as tiny as a sand crab that can make your eyes light up?

If not, look again.

Look at a child and you'll learn. Let them teach you how to find joy, how to be gleeful. The shining, smiling, skinny boy with the sand crab made an indelible impression on my soul. It is because of him that I gladly take the glee club oath: I will seek from this day forward to pull out the stops and give way to the merriment, mirth, gaiety, and exhilaration that is my birthright as a child of a gleeful God.

Will you join the club? A joy that is shared is doubled. That's why the boy came running and left leaping.

> "Truly I tell you, unless you change and become like children,
> you will never enter the kingdom of heaven."
> MATTHEW 18:3

Traveling Light

Let the burden be never so heavy, love makes it light.
ROBERT BURTON

He pulls out the small wheelchair from the trunk of the car. She holds the ever-growing frame of her child tenderly in her arms, awaiting the big "1, 2, 3, now" of their moving him from the car to the chair. They have this routine down pat. For seventeen years now they have lovingly moved their severely disabled child a dozen times a day in a world of upright, uptight people schooled in fast-paced impatience and bodily perfection.

In fine restaurants, in cathedrals, on beaches, and in lovely shops—all around the world, they carry him. They smile at him.

They love him.

My Japanese friends Mitsue and Takao travel the world, but never without their son Ryuji and the small wheelchair and the "1, 2, 3, now" routine that gives their lives so much meaning and joy. While many in their situation would neatly place their child with relatives while they travel, this couple dares to be different.

Now they have come to California for a visit, and we spend time together in all the tourist spots. As we stroll through theme parks and visit rocky beaches, I wonder what courage it must take to carry this child all over the world. But when I look at their lives, so joyful and rich, I see that they have created something immensely beautiful with this challenge. They have created a life of joy in the simplicity of a sweet, small head resting on their laps—a life swelled with Beauty's tenderness.

I help to hold Ryuji's head up so he can drink out of the water bottle. The day is hot, and the streets of Universal City Walk are crowded with teenagers who stand tall and straight, parents with children who are healthy and smiling. Beautiful people, yes, but I wonder, what is a beautiful life? Sitting here in the hot summer sun with this child and his loving parents, I realize that they are much happier and more carefree than so many parents I see who are scolding and arguing with their children.

I realize that a beautiful life comes not from sterile, perfect existence, but from taking what is and creating what can be. It's a kind of art that my friends have excelled in. An art I am learning in their graceful presence.

They have taught me without words that we have a choice in what we do with these ill-fitting pieces of life—a disability, a loss, a heartbreak, a pain that won't go away. We can choose to shrink back from life, let all joy dry up, and wither away into the netherworld of depression. Or we can embrace the fact of the situation and join hands with divine Beauty, who ravishes the universe with something more than our pain.

Whatever we have or don't have, we can create from it, if only we have the courage to say yes to the ever-tender Lover of all that is not quite right.

With God's empowerment we can create Beauty out of any situation, even when a "cure" is not possible. But God needs us.

God needs our courage.

As partners with God, we can bring about miracles of Beauty that transcend the world's expectations of perfection. A beautiful life is one that sees beyond the disabilities, the limitations, and the obstacles, and dares to risk the unusual. As my friends have taught me, if we dare to take love with us on the journey, there is no burden that cannot be made light; there is no limit to Beauty's gracefulness in the universe.

"For my yoke is easy, and my burden is light."
MATTHEW 11:30

Flying High

Love possesses seven hundred wings, and each one extends from the highest heaven to the lowest earth.

RUMI

It was a moment of ordinariness...

I stand here in the shade of a mobile building on the a campus where elementary school children are in serious play. It is recess. I have stepped in today to "shadow" Julie, an autistic child.

I have watched her eat her lunch—peanut butter sandwich, apple

60

juice, and red gummy sharks. Now I watch her swing. She's flying high, so high the recess teacher has to warn her to slow down!

No one else is on the swing set. Only Julie.

Her long blonde hair flying, her lean body arching into the wind, her stylish glasses—you would think she was like other children. But she eats alone, swings alone, and experiences a world that we don't quite understand.

As I watch her swing on that sunny, warm day, while children are screaming and scheming and giggling as children do, my heart is full of Julie. I watch her and pray. With every arc she carves in the blue sky, I pray more fervently. I worry about her future.

How will she make it?

Is it possible to be happy and alone? Perhaps she feels a connection with things that I can't see—imaginary, magical things. Maybe she feels bound to the wind and to the sky and knows they will hold her. But how will she make it in a world that demands our social interaction?

Watching her, it dawns on me. We are all handicapped in some way. We feel alienated at times because of things mysterious inside us.

In our human frailties, I think we are shadowed by a loving God under whose wing we can feel safe and connected. I think Julie must have a sense of that. Being under the shadow of God's wing we can freely fly, with a sense of liberation, even within our boundaries.

None of us is completely whole in the ideal sense. We have our demons and our wounds and holes in our hearts bigger than the Grand Canyon. But watching Julie fly high I realize that we do not have to be imprisoned by any of those things.

The key is not perfection but love.

A sense of being hovered over by tender love, shadowed by compassion, and held in Beauty's luminous embrace—this is necessary for Julie and for me and for everyone who wishes to fly high and stretch the boundaries of our humanity.

Standing there against the cool building, shadowing and praying and thinking of Beauty who takes us under her wing, I smile. The bell rings, and we're off.

It was a moment of ordinariness...with wings.

How precious is your steadfast love, O God!
All people may take refuge in the shadow of your wings.
PSALM 36:7

The Looney Kin

Neither the past nor the future can be erased; both impinge upon our presentness in an ambiguous mixture of loss and hope.

MARJORIE HEWITT SUCHOCKI

Genealogy. It's all the rage these days, and rightly so. We want to know from "whence we come" because it affects "whither we go." The more understanding we have of our roots, the more insightful our present and the more open our future. Knowledge of our past can be illuminating!

Of course, we may not always be bowled-over-thrilled with our findings.

My Aunt Mary Belle, the genealogist in our family, recently added another piece to the puzzle of our Adams family roots. While there are no Morticia, Lurch, or Cousin Itt characters lurking about in the shadows of our history, there is, much to my disappointment, no presidential legacy either. No Johns or Abigails. An ordinary lot, it appears to be.

But there is the most surprising—but on second thought, not so surprising—news. After having supper with Aunt Mary Belle, my sister, Lexy, e-mails me with the revelation:

"Did you know we have family members by the name of Looney? Does it surprise you?"

"It figures...certainly does explain some things," I e-mail back, smiling. "But I suppose it could be worse."

And it is.

She continues: "Mary Belle got all the birth and death certificates in her genealogy research, and one of the Looney's deaths was listed as 'eaten by a hog!'"

Well that does it. I don't want to know anything more about my Looney kin!

But the past won't let us forget. The past always impinges upon the present. What we do with the past determines which way we can go in the future. We have a choice relevant to the situation, no matter how many Looneys or hogs involved. In this case, Lexy and I choose to laugh and pass this story on because every family deserves a bit of fun. Now if the Looneys had also been ax murderers, we might have chosen a different response.

With regard to our personal pasts, it's the same. We need to know and embrace every part of ourselves—Looneys, hogs, and all—with compassion (and humor). In this way we open the door to new ways of seeing ourselves and the world. If we are embarrassed about the past or try to deny some shadowy part of ourselves that we just don't like, we will miss something important. Why not look our pasts straight in the face and see what kind of response will be most healing, most beautiful, most transforming for the most people? In this honest way, we offer to God our whole selves, which God then embraces, transforms, and opens up for new future paths of joy. In familiar language, it's all about forgiveness, healing, wholeness, and wisdom gained.

Our religious histories are ever present, too. Just look at the Bible. The glorious, the evil, the humorous, the embarrassing—it's all there for us! Stories of our faith are just as important and juicy as family histories. There is stubborn Jonah, who is spit out of the mouth of a whale, and Balaam, who is lectured to by a donkey, and Saul, who literally goes loony.

And then there are silly-headed, lazy disciples who fall asleep on the job or preach so long people start falling out of windows. Our ancestors, spiritual and physical, were all an imperfect, two-faced, hilarious lot. We need to study them, to know them as parts of ourselves. Only then can we work with God to carve out a freer, more joyous future for ourselves and our world. We may need to repent on behalf of our ancestors who did awful things in the name of religion or family. We may need to laugh or cry or just stand amazed by the courage we discover in others.

Some of that lives on in us.

Learn the stories of your roots, your faith, your family, your culture. Better yet, write down your own stories to pass down. And don't doll yourself up. Be real. If you're taken down by a hog, well, that's just the way it is. Nothing is lost in God. All of it is transformed into something fresh and good—and maybe even hilarious!

Abraham was the father of Isaac, and Isaac the father of Jacob, and Jacob the father of Judah and his brothers.
MATTHEW 1:2

Does God Ever Sleep?

God is in the world, or nowhere, creating continually in us and around us.

ALFRED NORTH WHITEHEAD

September 16, 2001.

Five-year-old Amanda shakes my hand on Sunday morning before going into worship with her usual beaming smile. But this time, instead of her usual "hello," she cuts through the preliminaries and simply asks, "Does God ever sleep?"

What a question! What a child.

Amanda, let me try to answer your question in light of our recent American tragedy. As you know, on September 11, very bad people did very bad things to our country, and we have all been sad. Some people might say that if God has ever gone to sleep, it must have been on September 11. We wonder why such bad things happen, how people can be so very bad! Where was God during all this? Was God asleep?

Amanda, God was not asleep. God never sleeps. God is too busy loving us and listening to us and hurting with us. On September 11, God's heart was broken, and it's hard to sleep when your heart is breaking.

God is always awake to your tiniest thoughts and biggest hurts. God is always awake to bad things because they hurt so much. God is always awake to your cries and your prayers. Whenever your mom and dad see you hurt, they hurt too. They feel your pain. God feels our pain as a heavenly parent and holds us close as a mom or dad.

No, Amanda, God never sleeps. God's eyes are always open to see your beautiful smile. And sometimes, maybe even a lot of times, there are tears in God's eyes.

Love is something precious that is always wide awake, no matter what. The Bible says, "God is love." God comes to us wide awake in the form of love, always love. Beware, Amanda, of anyone who does things "in the name of God" who does not love.

Don't worry, Amanda. God is never off taking a nap. Look around and you'll see God at work in lots of folks: moms and dads; people who pray; people who are kind; heroes such as firefighters, rescue workers, and brave people on airplanes.

Whenever you think God is sleeping, if you look in these places, you'll find God very much awake. This is where God lives and works without even yawning once.

Yes, Amanda, God is very much awake in people just like *you*.

God is love.
> 1 JOHN 4:16

Jasmines in Bloom

And this is all we can manage these days and also all that really matters: that we safeguard that little piece of You, God, in ourselves.

ETTY HILLESUM, 1942

We need our heroes.

There are three hardcover books stacked neatly—but not too neatly—on my nightstand. These books have nourished me for years. Some books are simply that rich. Three gems: Anne Morrow Lindbergh's *Gift from the Sea,* Rainer Maria Rilke's *Book of Hours,* and Etty Hillesum's *An Interrupted Life* continue to comfort and challenge me.

Of the three books, it is Etty's book that teaches me how to nourish Beauty within while coping with ugliness and terror on the outside. I call her "Etty" because by now, after all these years of reading her, she's like an old friend. Etty, a Dutch Jew, died in a death camp in 1943. But the diary she left behind will forever move me and countless others with an extraordinary way of looking at life, God, and the world.

She was inspired deeply by her Jewish heritage, as well as by the gospel of Matthew. Her spiritual mentor was the poet Rilke, and her spiritual practice was meditative prayer and writing. She was a true intellectual, a gifted writer, a lover of books and music—a true renaissance woman!

And my hero.

Etty dreamed of being a professional writer and was in love with a young protégé of Carl Jung. Etty's dreams died with her, but with her inner resources, Beauty grew, undaunted. And it lives on.

Etty believed in a beautiful God. She believed in jasmines. And this is how she prayed:

> The jasmine behind my house has been completely ruined by the rains and storms of the last few days, its white blossoms are floating about in muddy black pools on the low garage roof. But somewhere inside me the jasmine continues to blossom undisturbed, just as profusely and delicately as ever it did. And it spreads its scent round the House in which You dwell, oh God. You can see, I look after You, I bring You not only my tears and my forebodings on this stormy, grey Sunday morning, I even bring you scented jasmine. [1]

In the end she died. But she was not destroyed. The jasmines inside her would never quit blooming, and the God she cared about so tenderly would never cease needing her belief in jasmines. And everyone she touched felt her strength. And when she left one internment camp to go to her death in Auschwitz, she threw out a postcard from the train that was later found. It said, "We left the camp singing."

Etty teaches me how to embrace a beautiful God in unbeautiful times. She teaches me how to find jasmines in muddy pools of hate, terror, and death. Now, more than ever, we need her witness, her blooming. For unspeakable horror has knocked on our door too.

We need our heroes to support us and to lure us to the depth of things with their Beauty. Etty Hillesum—this lover of jasmines—is

---

[1] Etty Hillesum, *An Interrupted Life: The Diaries of Etty Hillesum* (New York: Pantheon, 1983), 152.

mine. Her life, the one she left on paper, helps me to embrace the present terror from an inner source of divine Beauty. Here we learn from a gifted hand that there is something more than ugliness, something indefatigable, yet fragile. Something that just keeps blooming.

Come what may.

> *The wilderness and the dry land shall be glad,*
> *the desert shall rejoice and blossom;*
> *like the crocus it shall blossom abundantly,*
> *and rejoice with joy and singing.*
> ISAIAH 35:1–2

A Tea Party of Unfinished Stories

Each friend represents a world in us, a world possibly not born until they arrive, and it is only by this meeting that a new world is born.

ANAIS NIN

Friends are like stories, unfinished tales that we help write. I have many different kinds of friends of all shapes, sizes, colors—and even species. Each friend is a whole world of fascinating tales (or tails as the case may be). Each person we encounter comes packed in his or her own story, and when we enter into friendship with that person, we unpack this story as we open ourselves to his or her world.

All my friends have stories—stories that inspire me, stories that intrigue me, stories that break my heart. And when I enter into them by simply sitting still and opening my heart, I become a little part of the story and perhaps, by my listening, influence which way the story will be played out.

Today I sit with some older, graceful friends, listening around a table of tea and butter cookies and chocolate candies to rich stories of long-lived lives. While pouring vanilla Ceylon tea from a rose-patterned English teapot, we pour out vignettes of days long past. Being the youngest present, I am all ears. Usually I can't wait to tell a story, but this afternoon I just want to listen and sip tea and eat butter cookies.

Listening hard with each sip of tea, I yearn to enter into each friend's world, into each world that opens up to the musical clink of china tea cups and tiny silver spoons. As one elderly woman tells her tale of the first time she saw a television set, I can almost see Milton Berle on that television. I can also hear her first gramophone and watch her dance the jitterbug! With another story, I feel the tinge of sadness in one's lost love. I realize as I grab the last chocolate orange stick that these special friends of mine have stories that just keep going and transmuting into glorious and sometimes tragic new chapters. But their stories—triumphant, humorous, or sad—are always enveloped with a graceful taste of beauty, faith, and love that made everything somehow all right and somehow not quite finished.

Good stories leave us yearning for more.

Listening to my gray-haired friends, I realize that our stories keep writing themselves, that there is always another chapter that can heal and transform. It takes age to see this sometimes. I believe God is the Creative Lure who pulls us onward into new chapters of possibilities. And we are cocreators in the writing.

The simple, stark, and sometimes traumatic stories of early experiences may come together in the end, weaving ever-deepening richness, softness, and understanding in adulthood. Unfinished business and loose ends come to completion in a new creative movement. In our divine/human storymaking, we may revisit a painful story and simply decide to be at peace with it, creating new spaces in our hearts for something fresh.

Sometimes the best way to deal with painful experiences from the past is simply to tell them as a story or write them down in a notebook and then let them be. Maybe we need to put a period where we have always left a comma. In the telling we free up energy to form another story with God's never-ending possibilities.

We need to share our stories.

Stories make lasting friendships and connect us with the Great Storyteller. The telling-listening-telling-listening is a gorgeous contrapuntal dance that unleashes ever-fresh divine possibilities.

The tea party of unfinished stories reveals to me a God who loves our stories, a God who writes best with butter cookies and laughter, a God who is not finished with our stories just yet. Friends of God don't judge and censor a story, but simply hear it spoken in its own voice so that the story might continue on in ways that are healing and grace-filled.

We are all unfinished stories, and we need our friends—and maybe a cup of tea—to help us write the next page. Which will it be: a drama? a love story? a saga of tragedy and triumph? We can't say for sure, and only in the telling will we find out. But one thing we do know: Our story is not finished. Whatever dark and painful elements keep popping up in our stories are only part of the story.

Let us wait until the whole thing is finished and find Beauty wrapping her love around it, like a friend offering a warm cup of tea on a very cold day.

Let anyone who has an ear listen.
REVELATION 13:9

Before the Bell Rings

Always forgive your enemies; nothing annoys them so much.
OSCAR WILDE

"We're revolting!" announce Lucy and Ethel, arms folded, chins in the air.

"No more than usual," respond Ricky and Fred.

Lucy and Ethel wanted "automatic dishwashers." They never did get the automatic dishwashers, but they did get a lot of laughs and my undying devotion. Lucy and Ricky, Fred and Ethel. Immortal. Beloved. They are my heroes in comedy. When I need to laugh, I turn to my stack of *I Love Lucy* videos that I have carefully taped and categorized over the years. I'm not sure there has ever been or ever will be any program that can match the genius of Lucy and her antics with Ethel.

I am watching the episode in which Fred asks Lucy to help him buy Ethel a birthday present. Lucy is delighted. Fred says that Ethel mentioned a toaster, but Lucy thinks a toaster is too boring and practical, and so she chooses for Ethel a pair of "smart party pants." Before her birthday, Ethel finds the package hidden in the closet and opens the package in Lucy's presence (thinking Fred had bought it). Lucy is ready to explode with gleeful anticipation as Ethel unwraps the gift. As the pants come out of the package, Ethel lets out a sigh that could wilt a field of tulips. She balks at the gaudy, impractical pants (and they are pretty ugly), laughing at Fred's awful taste, and says that what she *really* wants is a toaster.

Predictably, Lucy's feelings are hurt, and thus ensues one of a million classic fights between Lucy and Ethel. But of course, by the end of the show they are hugging and crying and making up as the best of friends. Whether the subject is the party pants, a bum washing machine, or little Ricky's drumming, the Mertzes and the Ricardos are always fighting and making up. Why it so easy for them to make up after all those hurt feelings?

Because they are like children, like the child in Fyodor Dostoyevsky's *The Brothers Karamozov* who says, "Papa, I'll throw him down when I'm big. I'll knock him down with my sword. I'll rush at him, throw him down, hold my sword over him and say: 'I could kill you now, but I forgive you, so there!'"

Like children, Lucy and Ethel choose the need for friendship over the need to be right. Isn't it that way with children? You see them on the playground fighting, and a few minutes later they're back in the sandbox together again as if nothing had happened. Yes, Lucy and Ethel are insanely childish, but they are delightfully childlike as well. They know how to make up quickly, like children on a playground who have only so much time for recess.

I think God must suffer because of our need to be right. Stone-cold "rightness" at the expense of relationships may indeed be for fundamentalists in religion or for egoists in academia. But that kind of righteousness has no place in Beauty's sphere. Beauty is strong enough and big enough to handle contrasts and conflicts in its hugeness. Beauty is flexible and forgiving and puts love above all things.

Watching Lucy and Ethel reminds me that Beauty is always on the side of forgiveness, mercy, and friendship. It also reminds me that life is short.

So make up…before the bell rings.

"Forgive us our debts, as we also have forgiven our debtors."
MATTHEW 6:12

PART 4

Embracing Beauty in Imagination and the Arts

*"Beauty is truth, truth beauty,"—
that is all Ye know on earth, and all
ye need to know.*

JOHN KEATS,
"ODE TO A GRECIAN URN"

Mexican Food, Mozart, and More

There is a deep mystery in life—something more—and it is good.

JAY MCDANIEL

I shouldn't have eaten the spicy enchiladas with hot sauce right before the concert. My stomach is reeling; my insides are on fire; and I think, *I'm not going to make it...I may have to leave during the concert.* Instead of enjoying the program notes, I'm lambasting myself for eating green sauce, on this of all nights, and debating how to handle this situation.

I've been waiting for this "Mostly Mozart" concert for weeks. And here I am feeling sick and distracted and miserable.

The concertmaster appears on stage, and my anxiety rises with the applause. Eyeing the Exit signs, I panic inside, *It's too late to leave now...and I'm stuck in the middle of the row and will have to climb over half a dozen people to get out...Should I try to take another antacid right now, without water? But then I might choke and really disrupt things.*

The Maestro enters, bows, and takes his place. All is still but the ethereal sound of a solo violin against the deep, dark silence of Segerstrom Hall.

And the magic of Mozart begins.

Almost instantly, my stomach takes a backseat to the music. The universe within me suddenly opens up to include more than my worrisome physical condition. There is a haunting beauty that pervades the place, a feeling that something besides pain—yes, something positively glorious—is afoot in the world!

The burning in my stomach is still present, but receding in importance as this effervescent, witty phenomenon called Mozart steals my heart for the evening. There is a settling down, a release of tension and pain, a letting go to something more than my personal discomfort. This sudden experience of spaciousness in the midst of an acute attack of indigestion sings of life itself.

I'm reading an intriguing book by Jay McDaniel, who writes, "Faith is a trustful letting go, in which we open out into the divine mystery and feel included in a larger whole. It is trust in Open Space."

Jay encourages me to see "something more" than my pain, as real as that pain may be. He writes:

> My name for this moreness, of course, is God. For God is the encircling presence, shining through a dark and starlit sky, within which all things are small but included: the stars and planets, the hills and rivers, the joys and sorrows. Faith, then, is making contact with God by means of trust. It is a trustful letting go, in which something goes wide in our hearts, and we see into the Open Space, gaining perspective on our lives.[1]

In this particular moment, my letting go into this Open Space that is God means letting go into Mozart. I feel in this moment like Edna St. Vincent Millay when she says, "I am waylaid by Beauty." It is too powerful for me. I have no choice but to succumb.

I think of Mozart the man, who lived an appallingly tragic life and was buried in a pauper's grave at the age of thirty-five. He was often vain and childish. But when he wrote music, he transcended his personal pain and human flaws by letting go to this "something more." His music was pure, honest, full of the stuff of life: laughter and sorrow, tragedy and triumph. Tragedy is transformed in Beauty, the sorrowful movements moving out into the wider ocean of the completed sense of redemptive Beauty. Mozart's heart "went wide" whenever he penned his notes, and we, the hearers—the lucky ones—join him in this spacious feeling of the "something more" when we let go in trust to the Open Space.

Will we let go to this *something more*?

I did. I let go to the Open Space of this wide, gracious moment in time, and my pain lessened. No climbing over people, no stepping on toes, no embarrassment. The encircling presence absorbed my anxiety and transformed my suffering in this singular moment with Beauty's fierce power.

The Open Space calls us to let go into something beyond our pain. When we experience pain or fear of any kind, from heartburn

---

[1]Jay McDaniel, *Living from the Center* (St. Louis: Chalice Press, 2000), 130.

to an uncertain future, we need to hold on tightly to this promise of "moreness."

And if we can trust in this spacious mystery, we will see that our fears and pain and sorrows find a place in the transforming music of God's own wide, wide heart.

For now we see in a mirror, dimly, but then we will see face to face. Now I know only in part; then I will know fully, even as I have been fully known.
1 CORINTHIANS 13:12

Starry Night

I believe in the night.

RAINER MARIA RILKE

"Do stars have points?"

Of course they do! Well, not really.

It catches you off guard. The answer could go either way. I am a substitute teacher today in third grade. Mrs. Thompson leaves this simple question on the board for the children to ponder. I'm perplexed. I don't know what to tell the students. The answer is yes if it's an art lesson, but no if it's a science lesson. I try to make this clear to third graders who aren't really interested in complicated explanations.

"Mrs. Farmer, stars have five points," declares chubby Jose, with little fat cheeks framing a confident third-grade smile.

"I get gold stars on my homework when my mom signs it," says Claribell.

Who am I to mess with their minds?

"Well, here it is," I say. "Some stars in the sky aren't really there."

Blank stares. Some downright hostile looks.

"The light from those stars is still there, though. Artists through the centuries have tried to depict light with points that draw the light from the center outward…blah, blah, blah."

Even I am suspicious of this substitute teacher's explanation. Then a substitute teaching miracle happens. Like a divine epiphany,

I see it on the back wall: a colorful art print on a bulletin board below a display sign that says, "The Great Masters." The miracle rescue is, of course, Vincent van Gogh's *The Starry Night*. And the rest is...art.

Muddying up science with art and my personal commentary– God forgive me. I can do no other. I'll wait for Mrs. Thompson to come back and straighten them out.

All I know is, the starry sky holds our dreams. True, some of the stars are not actually there. But their light is there, and that's all we need. It's all the wise men needed. In our spiritual lives we need to have stars in our night to take us out of the ordinary and into the dream world of what is possible.

In the powerful movie *A Beautiful Mind*, we cannot forget Jennifer Connelly's imploring face and searing words when faced with her husband's illness: "I have to believe that something extraordinary is possible." This yearning is the essence of everything meaningful in our spiritual journey. This is what stars do in their twinkling. They tell us that something extraordinary is possible.

God is like the starry night. I can't think of a better picture of what Alfred North Whitehead calls "the Lure of God" than a starry night. The starry night lures us to think big, twinkling, mysterious thoughts. The starry sky is hugely alluring, like van Gogh's painting, pulling us toward all that is good and true and extraordinarily beautiful.

Perhaps mixing together science, art, theology, and Jose's five-point theory–like paints on a palette–is a good thing after all. In *A Beautiful Mind*, something extraordinary does, indeed, happen. It all begins when mathematical genius John Nash, played by Russell Crowe, points to the stars with a lovely dark-haired student who believes in the stars and in him. In his later years, after a long battle with schizophrenia, he stands triumphantly and humbly to accept a Nobel Prize with words you wouldn't really expect from a mathematical wizard. He says he has discovered in his quest for logic that "the mysteries of love are where logic is found."

Love, science, starry nights, logic–it all gets mixed up and swirled around until something extraordinary emerges. That's what Beauty does. That's what God does in the divine, sparkling, unending storehouse of fresh possibilities. There is always a new star for every moment. It may have five points like Mrs. Thompson's gold stars. It may be circular, strange, and wild, like van Gogh's stars. But the thing is, God never runs out of stars, out of beautiful possibilities for the next moment.

No matter how ugly and confusing and dreary the daylight, when the twinkling stars come out at night, we know that something extraordinary is up ahead.

We just know it.

That's God's job—to keep us dreaming, to lure us as a Lover to actualize all those things that are not there...yet. We just need to look up and let the stars pull us in, so that our dreams are constantly and eternally bathed in Beauty's warmth and light.

> *"I will indeed bless you, and I will make your offspring as numerous as the stars of heaven and as the sand that is on the seashore."*
> GENESIS 22:17

Walking with Hemingway

Like a potter shaping clay at her wheel,
sound shapes and sculpts us both inside and out.

DON CAMPBELL

Tonight I walked with Hemingway.

I love to walk and listen to books though my headphones, and hear words rise and fall into space like musical notes. Each vowel and consonant is like a note making up stanzas of words. It's musical if done right. And Hemingway does it right.

There are very few American writers I admire more than Ernest Hemingway. I don't personally care for some of his subject matter, such as bullfights and boxing, but the man can write, and I am captivated, even if I have to fast-forward through a bullfight.

His book *The Sun Also Rises* reminds me of *The Great Gatsby*, written by his good friend F. Scott Fitzgerald. They wrote about their generation—the one Gertrude Stein named "The Lost Generation"—those who lived between the two world wars. Their characters are too wealthy, too idle, and way too full of angst to be liked. But the writers somehow manage to bring together words that create Beauty in the very midst of the impoverished souls they wrote about.

It's amazing, really, what they can do with words.

Through words we find all kinds of redemption. "In the beginning was the Word," we know from the gospel. I especially like the spoken word, such as listening to scripture being read in worship by a well-prepared reader or listening to Hemingway being read on a cassette tape. Words do have power when they hit the air. Try to imagine reading a manuscript by Martin Luther King, Jr., without thinking of his voice. It's hard to do. We hear him. We need to hear him.

Books by great authors are worth reading aloud or listening to with headphones on a long walk. We need more storytellers and teachers and preachers who care about the way words wrap around us in tone and timbre. We need to hear the words melt into the air of our imaginations. We need to hear subtle nuances of emotion. We need to see the colors of the words as they pass by, one by one. We need to know the textures and the way the words bounce or fling themselves about in the night air, or in a classroom, or in a place of worship. All this changes us.

That's why we need to read aloud to children and adults alike. Maybe even to ourselves. To sit by a bed in the hospital and read *Harry Potter* to a child may be the most healing action we can perform, because the spoken word is powerful. And we participate in this power when we read a story aloud.

Divine Beauty is always moving in time, "ripening," as Rainer Maria Rilke would say. I see Beauty unfolding most vividly in sound. Think of how music unfolds, note by note, phrase by phrase, rising and falling into space until time is filled up with a symphony in sound. The same is true for words as we listen to them. Whether a vibration in the air is the sonorous sound of a clarinet or the deft words of Hemingway, we know there is something magical afoot in the world.

It's a powerful thing to be in the path of vibrating Beauty.

The liveliness of God is heard in words that are three-dimensional, round and full-bodied. These are spoken words, as the first stories of humankind were passed on. And each telling has its own special power.

Reading is good. But hearing words in the mystery of their unfolding bears special archetypal power that we are only on the verge of understanding. Reading aloud resembles most clearly the way God works in the world. Not in a static, flat, one-dimensional way like words on a page, where we can flip to the end of the book and find out what happens. No, God works in the unfolding nuances of the moment, with a book that is always in the process of being written in a dynamic coauthorship between God and the world.

Walk with a great author. Read a book aloud and let the words spill into the air. Let words ripen in sound and be tasted by a world that is always in need of a delicious, satisfying story.

"Let anyone with ears to hear listen!"
MARK 4:23

An Antidote for Stupidity

He who binds to himself a joy
does the winged life destroy.
But he who kisses the joy as it flies
lives in eternity's sunrise.

WILLIAM BLAKE

Is it possible to eat too much chocolate? A no-brainer, you would think. But I—one who likes to question all things and break the rules sometimes—decided to put it to the test. My inspiration came from watching for the umpteenth time the *I Love Lucy* episode "The Candy Factory" (the one where Lucy and Ethel go to work for the "Chocolate Nazi").

Watching Lucy and Ethel cram chocolate into their mouths at the speed of light made me wonder how much we can stretch the body's capacity for sheer foolishness. Determined to beat Lucy's and Ethel's world record for the most chocolate stuffed in the mouth at one time, I had to find out for myself the limits of human stupidity. (It was also an excuse to polish off leftover Valentine's Day candy.)

So, armed with a huge, heart-shaped box of chocolates, a Saturday to myself, and a string of old movies to watch, I began the experiment. Ignoring the few rational thoughts that tried to enter my head, I ate one crème-filled chocolate after another.

The results of my experiment were frightful. Yes, I concluded, after half a bottle of an antacid and a desire to take a baseball bat to my own head, you *can* eat too much chocolate. Oh, don't we love to test the limits of our foolishness?

I learned something from this ridiculous experiment. I learned that things we love can make us sick. Foolishness is taking something perfectly wonderful, such as chocolate, and being perfectly stupid with it. When I think about the things I love to excess besides chocolate, the list is daunting. Lipstick is probably next to chocolate on my list. I buy and hoard new lipsticks that I don't ever use when at least half the world is malnourished. That's not a good thing.

We bind ourselves to a lot of things and inner states of mind that are simply destructive to ourselves and impoverishing to others. Put philosophically, foolishness is part of the human situation. We take delicious, wonderful things, such as chocolate or friendship or wine or even religion, and grasp them so tightly to us that we get sick and hurt ourselves and those around us. Our lovely desires can turn into nightmares.

That's the bad news.

But the good news is that there is an antidote for stupidity. A single line from a poem by the Romantic poet, William Blake: "He who kisses the joy as it flies lives in eternity's sunrise."

Do you see the possibilities here? Kiss the joy as it flies; don't cling to it insanely.

Binding yourself to any good thing will weigh you down like Jabba the Hut in chains (which is how I felt after the chocolate experiment). You will do stupid things, believe me.

Clinging causes suffering. A Buddhist nun in Ohio taught me this truth on a bone-chilling day in January. I remember it (though, obviously, not all the time).

Kissing the joy as it flies is possible when we know that God experiences our joys with us and saves them for all eternity. When we think that our lives are meaningless wisps of air, we try to cling and grab and hoard everything. But when we settle into the notion of a generous God who is with us, gathering up the delicious moments for all eternity, then we can relax and let go to God's never-ending joy. We relax into the source of all these joys, the Beauty of God.

Isn't this what we really want anyway? Every good and delicious thing is a glimmer of divine Beauty—something to be kissed, savored, and fully experienced, but not clung to.

Meditation, centering prayer, journaling, or writing poetry are some practices that help free us from the excesses of clinging to our natural and good desires. Spiritual disciplines in the contemplative tradition help us to hold things lightly.

Lightly, not tightly. That is Beauty's secret.

Delicious, beautiful moments are all saved and will come again in fresh packages because we are forever bound to a delicious, beautiful God. A beautiful, spacious, generous God is the only thing worth binding ourselves to. All other things are merely poor substitutes.

So take a lesson from Lucy, Ethel, and me. Let that chocolate go.

"But strive first for the kingdom of God...and all these things will be given to you as well."
MATTHEW 6:33

Vivaldi Uncorked

The art of progress is to preserve order amid change,
and to preserve change amid order.
ALFRED NORTH WHITEHEAD

Today I'm ready to wrap a glorious piece of music around my soul: *The Four Seasons.* You know this. It's not a hotel. It's not a pop group from the 1960s. It is one of the hidden treasures from the eighteenth century. The glorious concerto by Antonio Vivaldi is a masterpiece, but it often only serves as background music in fine restaurants or at expensive department stores.

I believe the world of art and music is a world in which Beauty weaves some of her most exquisite garments. There is a whole world inside books and films and music and art galleries that can transmute our mundane lives into intensely satisfying experiences. But the arts often seem inaccessible, sterile, as if they belong in another world.

Violinist Ann-Sophie Mutter is one of those artists who know how to bridge the gap between inaccessible music and the deepest yearnings of our decidedly nonclassical generation. Mutter is often called the goddess of classical music by a new generation of hungry listeners who want to transcend the ills and banalities of this life with feeling that touches the soul so deeply it hurts.

It wasn't long ago that Mutter's controversial and wildly popular interpretation of *The Four Seasons* splashed into the music world as a glorious celebration of life—wrinkled-nose critics aside. Here I go, listening to this new interpretation for the first time, with headphones in place, as I walk around the track at the park near my home.

Fellow walkers, move aside! I'm not looking at anything or even aware of my feet touching the ground. Captivated wholly by Beauty's feeling in sound, the world is suddenly transformed.

Why all the fuss over this chamber work from the Baroque period? Most interpretations of this work are stolid, beautiful, and devotional in quality, like High Mass. Mutter's new version is, as one critic put it, "the popping of vintage champagne corks—a high spirited celebration." It seems, somehow, to resonate with a new generation that thought "Baroque" meant something that needed to be fixed.

Would the composer *like* this "uncorked" interpretation of his work? I don't know. But my feeling is that divine Beauty *dances* with it. I sense, in Mutter's playing, a lively trio: Vivaldi, Mutter, and God. This is the way it should be. Passion leaps out of the music and begins dancing with an exuberance that can only erupt from the Spirit of Life!

This fresh interpretation has captivated the attention of young people who don't buy tickets to the symphony, who thought they hated classical music. No longer dead and antiquated, or simply "music for the rich," Vivaldi's art—still holding its original integrity—now becomes an eternally growing, living thing thanks to Anne-Sophie Mutter.

What if Mutter's strategy were applied to other things in Beauty's treasure trove? A "dead" or even oppressive-sounding passage of scripture might come to life with a fresh interpretation that evokes freedom for the hearer. My husband, a biblical scholar in the tradition of process theology, writes, "The meaning of a text is open-ended, evolving with the creative advance of the world."[1] Ah, how liberating

---

[1]Ronald L. Farmer, *Beyond the Impasse: The Promise of a Process Hermeneutic* (Macon, Ga.: Mercer University Press), 105.

for us all! And this applies to all texts, even if they are made up of sound or color rather than words. Any treasure from the past must constantly be allowed to live and breathe and grow through loving interpretation that is both respectful of the past and alive to the present.

We often have bipolar disorder when it comes to past treasures. On one extreme, we want to eradicate the past because it no longer seems relevant. On the other extreme, we want to preserve the past in a sterile casket, without the lively freshness and relevance it needs for the changing world in which we live.

Mutter's musical offering suggests another way, the way of transforming the rich brilliance of the past into fresh interpretations for the present as cocreators with the living God. If we are to transform our world, our communities of faith, our own lives, we need to embrace the treasures of the past and savor them, study them, love them, and re-create them as offerings to a beautiful God.

Bravo Anne-Sophie!

> *I will sing a new song to you, O God;*
> *upon a ten-stringed harp I will play to you.*
> PSALM 144:9

The Sky Artist

> *We must not portray you in king's robes,*
> *you drifting mist that brought forth the morning.*
>
> RAINER MARIA RILKE

Only in Southern California can you look up on a warm spring day and find a myriad of very unusual things. There is, of course, the story of the man who was seen flying over LAX in his lawn chair with hundreds of helium balloons attached (true story). But in my own piece of the world there are slightly less amazing things parading in the sky, nevertheless incredible to my eyes.

This afternoon on a simple walk, I look up and see a kite overhead daring the wind, higher and higher, as we cheer it on. And then as I watch the long-tailed kite disappear into the heavens, a huge smiley face catches my eye. Cloud formations? A miracle? Lucy in the Sky with Diamonds? Wait a minute. Let me blink a few times and try this again. Yes, it is definitely a smiley face. Maybe God is "smiling down on us" (even though we know that God is everywhere, not just pie in the sky by and by). Just then, I see the beginnings of a heart, first one half, then the other. A little lopsided, but definitely a heart. And it's in the sky.

Let me get my glasses.

OK, there is a rational explanation for all this. I see it now, a teeny tiny little airplane in the sky making us smile with the miracle of water vapors and a very skillful splash of cleverness on the pilot's part. Twisting and turning, rolling and diving—gosh, I hope the pilot didn't have Taco Bell chalupas for lunch.

But in this crazy, hugely impressive artwork in the sky, I imagine that I do see God smiling on us, not because we're good and kind (which is highly debatable), but because God's face is beautiful and God's nature is full of heart. I imagine this beautiful God with heart calling us to our true destiny in this world—to create huge smiles and slightly lopsided hearts on the sky canvas of our lives.

That old image of god-in-the-sky who is about as approachable as the Queen of England suddenly vanishes as the sky artist paints the warm, intimate, and vulnerable nature of my God, who numbers the hairs on my head.

How shall I be different after witnessing this marvel in the sky?

I shall with all my heart seek to be a sky artist, daring to draw the face of God, however imperfect, however dangerous, for the sake of Beauty, for the love of a world in need of heart. I give myself to it—a whirl, a turn, a twist, and even a roll here and there, imagining with my small craft a sky that smiles. Oh, just to create, even for a single moment, a simple picture of God's Beauty and Loving-kindness toward all creation! And when the vapors have disappeared, and I am gone, God will still remember. And others behind me will continue to create with God a sky parade that will keep us looking upward, hoping, praying, wondering, smiling.

The heavens are telling the glory of God;
and the firmament proclaims God's handiwork.
PSALM 19:1

Classical Healing

Music: the breathing of statues. Perhaps: the silence of
paintings. Language where language ends. Time that stands
head-up in the direction of hearts that wear out.

RAINER MARIA RILKE

Beauty nourishes. Body and soul.

In Madeleine L'Engle's graceful novels, she creates richly textured characters who often find healing from the tragedies of life through music. One of her most appealing protagonists is Katherine Vigneras, a retired concert pianist who, despite her successful career, suffered personally during the war in a Nazi camp and later the loss of a child. Through all her sufferings, she finds solace and personal grounding in music. And when she is old she tells her young protégé, "There are no guarantees that there will be no accidents or no evil or no pain. I can promise one thing only, and that is, your music will always see you through anything that happens, and that is no small promise."[1]

L'Engle's characters find in classical music "an affirmative structure in a world becoming daily more structureless."[2] I know this to be true.

In December 1999, right before Christmas, I was lying in an intensive care unit of a hospital hooked up to all kinds of gadgets. My doctor had just left. He told me that I was "not out of the woods yet," but I was better. I felt strengthened by this visit, yet still afraid. Terribly afraid. Noises, loud piercing buzzers, and high-tech alarms jarred me at every turn in my thoughts. But when my husband put on my headphones that allowed me to drown out the harsh noises with the sounds of Mozart, I felt the "structure" L'Engle speaks of. It held me and soothed me. This music—by a composer whose music Salieri said was "God's voice incarnate"—floated into my body and mind with such lightness and clarity and opaque beauty that I began to heal quickly and dramatically. There is no question in my mind that Mozart served

---

[1]Madeleine L'Engle, *A Severed Wasp* (New York: Farrar, Straus and Giroux, 1982), 370.
[2]Madeleine L'Engle, *A Live Coal in the Sea* (New York: Farrar, Straus and Giroux, 1996), 42.

as one facet of my healing, a divine touch, a prayer in sound, a nourishing balm to my cells and to my soul.

And I am not alone. Not long after my recovery I met a woman—much older than I—who came of out of a coma with the help of Mozart. Her first thoughts were of Mozart's music, and it brought her into the world again, healthy and whole. What joy we had sharing our stories!

We can depend on Beauty to see us through whatever we are experiencing because divine Beauty—in all its manifestations—lures us toward our deeper connections to life, health, and well-being. And here I'm speaking particularly of Beauty's music. Music—God incarnate in sound—unfolds with feelings too deep for words. Sometimes it is the very form of Beauty our bodies most yearn for.

We need, on a daily basis, an affirmative structure in which to feel alive and centered. This may be silent meditation, prayer, walking, or gardening. I urge you to add classical music to your healing and centering resources.

Plato said, "Rhythm and harmony find their way into the inward places of the soul." The trick is to find which music best fits the need we have at the moment. When it comes to healing and restoring, the steady structure and gentle melodies of the Baroque and Classical periods seem to work best. So add a bit of Bach, Vivaldi, Albinoni, Pachelbel, or Mozart to your day. Dare to delve into the riches of the past to find healing for the present.

And this is the exciting part: Not only will you find yourself centered in a deeper harmony, you will then—unconsciously—radiate this harmony to the world. Because of the astonishingly subtle connections to all things, you will change the world around you by simply listening to a piece of music! Inner harmonies are sweetly contagious.

The world, and sometimes our own bodies, seem out of our control. We feel unsettled, fearful, scattered. In the midst of all this undoing we need to find inside us a place of structured Beauty that is like a Bach fugue: balancing, whole, reasonable, pure.

We cannot always know the path our healings will take. We are mortal. Music can help us accept even this by luring us toward something more—something deep and trustworthy and eternally beautiful. In our eternal healing we are tenderly enfolded into a new melody—with harmonies that include all—in a symphony of God's creative, transforming composition.

So be a fugue. Be a sonata, a hymn, a concerto, or maybe a grand symphony. Become one with the music. Let it enter you as divine Spirit and hold you in its structure that is affirmative of an eternally beautiful God.

> *And whenever the evil spirit…came upon Saul, David took the lyre and played it with his hand, and Saul would be relieved and feel better, and the evil spirit would depart from him.*
> 1 SAMUEL 16:23

Evening News Blues

Humankind cannot bear very much reality.
T. S. ELIOT

The world is going to hell in a handbasket. Or so it seems when I turn on the evening news. Honestly, it seems as if we might as well throw in the towel rather than work for peace and justice. I curse the television. This insanity unleashed like a mad dog is too brutal for my sense of reality. It's more like a movie. Except this horrific story cannot seem to find an ending.

When I see the chaos of the Middle East and terror literally exploding all over the world, I wonder what I can do to cope and to help. What can I do to bring about Beauty in this hideous, ugly, brutal situation that seems too far out of control?

I turn on the radio. I find great solace in classical music, so I turn to my favorite classical station. But at this particular time I hear no music, but an advertisement for a new CD, not even a classical CD. I hear rock singer Sting talking about a new love song he's written for the romantic movie *Kate and Leopold.* He says, "In times like this, a love song is the most political thing you can do—really necessary."

He had already given the world the moving song "Fragile" right after the massive terrorist attack on our country. In this poignant music, he sings so sweetly and sadly, "On and on the rain will fall/

like tears from a star." It is a beautiful song. A healing song. But then he starts writing love songs as the next step in healing. He views this not as an escape from reality, but as something that makes a difference. It is political, he says.

I think he's on to something.

The "Evening News Blues" oddly turns into a love song. Somehow this makes it possible for me to bear a little more reality. Some of the most beautiful music and artwork and writings were produced during the dark days of World War II. As was the case then, we now have at our disposal a dark background on which to write a light and lovely song, or paint a yellow daisy, or maybe even pen a shining poem in silver and white.

Perhaps writing a love song is the thing we should do. We might write it with music or words or create a garden of whispy, fragile, dancing poppies.

On the six-month anniversary of the World Trade Center disaster, artists came together to create such a "love song" in the form of the Twin Lights Memorial to represent hope and light in the darkness where the Twin Towers had been. How powerfully moving to our spirits! Simple, pure lights, heaving hope clear up to the crying stars.

Whatever way we can write a love song to the world, we need to do it. It reminds us that love is stronger than death. It will help us bear the reality, and in that bearing, transform it. Despair only leads to more despair. We need to do something–anything–that sings of love.

We need to help God and the world by writing a love song.

"War is hell," the saying goes. What we need to do is to create some piece of heaven in this hell, not to escape, but to add a new ingredient to the mix, a new color, a new thing. War is the opposite of Beauty. It is intensity of feeling gone mad.

We all seek to feel intensely. It is how God made us. We know this as we flock to movies that make us cry and to roller coasters that scare the living daylights out of us; to sporting events and to people who make us feel alive and fresh. But hatred, war, and violence are also intense feelings, the kind that arise when there is a void of good feelings to thrive on–when there is not enough joy, music, or justice.

Let us keep this in our hearts as we sigh over the news, as we pray over the day's disasters. Let us seek in our offerings of Beauty something of justice and joy for all people and all creatures of the world, something simple and pure and intensely satisfying to our weary spirits.

Something like a love song.

Set me as a seal upon your heart,
  as a seal upon your arm;
for love is strong as death,
  passion fierce as the grave.
                    SONG OF SOLOMON 8:6

God's Wild Imagination

It is at the level of imagination that any full engagement
with life takes place.

AMOS WILDER

God has an imagination.

And out of this wild imagination comes just the right story, an autobiography of sorts—not the kind that tells all, but rather, one that offers a glimpse of how God thinks and feels and suffers and dreams in the world. Jesus of Nazareth is the main character of this story. It is not God's only story. God has many stories, but this one tells us something no other story tells. This is the story I know best.

In this story, Jesus is a storyteller himself, always spinning yarns about a tree or a mustard seed or a sad person on the road. He just looks around and creates stories that change people's lives. But the religious folk don't much understand his stories. Even more irritating to the self-righteous, law-abiding folk around him is the fact that he bucks the system, heals people when he's not supposed to, and has the audacity to raise the dead! He even declares sins forgiven and captives set free.

This does not go over well.

And to add insult to injury, he honors women and stands up for them, which really goes against the grain of his world. In fact, he likes children, lepers, prostitutes, tax collectors, and anyone who is shunned by society. How outrageous!

He's poor and doesn't have any financial security. He doesn't care. What he does care about is seeing people made whole in body and mind and spirit. He gets visibly angry at the people who think they know everything but who know nothing about what's important. He gets himself crucified by these people who are offended by his goodness and childlike love. He forgives them, even as he dies on the cross.

I cry at the climax of the story and wish it had a different ending.

And it does. It's one of those surprise endings, a twist that no one really anticipates. The same women Jesus loved so much had the joy of giving us the first inkling of this ending. They find his tomb empty! God's story ends in surprise and joy. Jesus is somehow, in some way, in some form, alive!

But there is still more.

Jesus lives in Spirit and continues to create within us stories that heal and make whole. God has many stories. I am one of those stories, and so are you. Other faith communities have their stories. All these add richness, depth, and wonder to this imaginative, storytelling God.

The story of Jesus is a story that never ends, really, as long as you and I dare to use our own imaginations to create some tender Beauty in the world. And it takes imagination to do this in our troubled world the way he did in his—loving all, excluding none, forgiving and making whole. It's a simple message, but not an easy one. Ask Gandhi. Ask Martin Luther King, Jr. It's beautiful. It's simple.

It's hard. It's what Alfred North Whitehead would call "tragic beauty."

Beauty is not always easy to create—not easy at all—especially now. How do we cope with our feelings of revenge and bitter hatred toward those who have violated us and our homeland? We need God's stories. We need this story. We need to wrestle with it and with ourselves.

And no matter what happens in this world, if we keep this story alive in our hearts, something surprising will emerge. And in the end, just when we think life is going to be a three-hanky ending, we can remember God's story in Jesus of Nazareth and imagine the wonder of Beauty's next rising!

Jesus told the crowds all these things in parables; without a parable he told them nothing.
MATTHEW 13:34

91

Van Gogh's God

I always think that the best way to know God is to love many things.

VINCENT VAN GOGH

Standing in a room full of paintings by Vincent van Gogh is a religious experience if ever there was one. When the van Gogh exhibit from Holland came to Los Angeles, nothing could stop me from being there. It was a pilgrimage.

Standing in the midst of self-portraits and peasants and crows and flowers—color and light and simplicity—I wondered as my heart took a leap: What was the inspiration behind this red-haired man of mystery, myth, and madness?

I bought a book at the museum bookstore called *Van Gogh and God* to see if I could unravel the mystery. And in this book author Cliff Edwards remarks that Vincent van Gogh's God has many parallels with the God of Alfred North Whitehead's "process philosophy."[1] (Ah! My dearest philosopher and this glorious artist in one breath! Things are starting to make sense.)

Whitehead's philosophy paints a picture of a tender God, creatively alive within all things, offering richly textured possibilities for Beauty in an evolving universe. So it is with van Gogh's canvasses of color and light. A tender, earthy love imbued with vulnerability and mystery—this is the essence of van Gogh's art. It is interesting that Vincent (as he preferred to be known) embraced a true religious experience only when he gave up the calling to the ministry, a calling he associated with a narrow view of God, and began to open up "to love many things."

Vincent looked to a God beyond the usual lawgiver model of his day, to one who is Love incarnate in the world. He says in a letter to his brother Theo, "What a mystery life is, and love is a

---

[1]Cliff Edwards, *Van Gogh and God: A Creative Spiritual Quest* (Chicago: Loyola University Press, 1989), 72.

mystery within a mystery. It certainly never remains the same in a literal sense, but the changes are like the ebb and flow of the tide, which leaves the sea unchanged."

The love in this man's heart was juxtaposed with pain from his mental illness. But it was in this disharmony—this very imperfection—that Vincent took hope in a future that was full of possibility. Imperfection in his illness and in the larger flawed creation of human pain was part of what he saw God to be: the vulnerable Struggling Artist in the process of creating a universe of Beauty.

When Vincent pledged himself to be an artist in 1880, he had surely left behind the "God of the clergyman"—the same God that Nietzsche proclaimed dead—and turned to this more expansive view of God, a God who loved many things. In this transforming image, van Gogh's God becomes intimately vulnerable and, at the same time, a mystery that lures us into the depth of things.

I look again at his art, this time with new eyes. I see both aspects of his God in his paintings—the earthy simplicity of peasants in a field and yet the dreaminess of his work that is without detail. This God of both concrete personal experience and dreamy mystery unfolds in color and light and texture.

The Struggling Artist needs van Gogh's vision of love. And mine too. And yours. We are all a part of it—this grand work of painting love in the world.

I feel a kinship with this man of mystery because his life was a quest for unification, a search for how to integrate the noblest ideas in religion with art, literature, and nature. His mental illness may have taken his life much too soon, but what he left behind only grows more powerful as lagging human sensitivity to divine tenderness catches up to Vincent's own.

His art speaks to us. No, it shouts out to us in color and light and texture and form: God is in *all* things! And so it is to all things we must give our love.

And now faith, hope, and love abide, these three; and the greatest of these is love.
1 CORINTHIANS 13:13

Between the Devil and the Deep Blue Sea

I have hymns you haven't heard.

RAINER MARIA RILKE

Life throws a lot of things at us. Sometimes it is more than we can bear.

And sometimes things are looking OK on the outside, but inside we feel trapped, like a caged animal. There seems to be no way out. No way at all.

What do we do when we feel trapped, when we feel caught between a rock and a hard place, or–my favorite–"between the devil and the deep blue sea"? I talked with a casual friend who was caught in such a dilemma. It was at the grocery store, and I had an appointment to get to. The "how are you?" turned into more than I wanted to know.

"I hate my job," she bemoaned.

"Well, why don't you quit?" I retorted, too easily, putting apples into my cart.

"I can't. Financially, I have to work."

"But you could find another job, surely," I said, edging toward the green beans.

"No, I'm not qualified for what I want."

"Well, then *get* qualified." I said, motioning tactfully that I needed the olive oil she was standing in front of.

"I can't..." And then came a hundred and one reasons.

Now I was the one feeling trapped! She was pushing me toward desperate acts such as filling my entire cart with Ben and Jerry's ice cream. Would she ever shut up so I could give her more simplistic advice and be on my way?

As the conversation continued, despite my annoyance, I realized sadly that she truly believed there was "no way out." Nothing I proposed lifted her spirits–nothing, nothing, *nothing* would work in her view.

Her despair troubled me as I finally got to the checkout stand, both because I was terribly insensitive to her plight and because I have no concept of "nothing." For me, there is always s*omething* new under the

94

sun because I worship a God who is full of abundant possibilities, a God of unending creativity and novelty, a God who resurrects something creative and hopeful in the midst of the worst situations.

I feel sorry for this woman, not because she hates her job, but because she doesn't believe in anything beyond her despair. If there is anything I believe in, it is that God's eternal vision is full of unrealized possibilities that we cannot imagine. Why not believe in that, even if nothing else seems plausible? Once we believe that God is truly on our side and that nothing is out of the realm of redemption—not even a dead-end job—then we can begin to imagine new things.

"Possibilities are because God is" says theologian Marjorie Suchocki. That's all we need to believe to avoid despair.

But all this said, it's still too easy to fall into despair when we just don't see or feel a way out. I have more sympathy for her than I let on. We've all felt trapped at some point in our lives, and it feels like hell. Sometimes we need a little encouragement to remind us that we will get out, that we will find another job, that our pain or loneliness or heartbreak will not last eternally, that God does, indeed, have songs we've never heard.

Thankfully, God has not only sympathy for our plight but empathy in the most intimate way. A beautiful God does not stand on the outside looking in. A beautiful God actually feels our feelings and knows our despair from the inside. It is Beauty's inner knowing that makes these divine possibilities tailor-made to the moment of our need. God is not the simplistic, know-it-all, casual friend who tells us to buck up while half listening. Our beautiful God is our companion in suffering and our empowerment to freedom.

There is a way out.

The next time you feel you are between the devil and the deep blue sea, avoid telling people at the grocery store. Find a friend who is not in a hurry.

And try this. Imagine your own dreams, your deepest desires. Let your vision of these dreams penetrate you and become a part of you, even if you only half believe it. Write it down. It helps to see your dreams on paper, in black and white, spelled out and clear and specific. Live with this dream, day after day, and watch it open up like a river into the vast ocean. Give God some help by believing in what seems now to be only a pipe dream.

But be careful with all this imagining. It may just scare the devil out of you!

Yes, God has hymns we haven't heard and dreams we haven't lived and hopes we haven't dared wish for. Beauty always offers a way out. Open yourselves to these fresh possibilities and find yourself sailing on the deep blue sea.

> *I am about to do a new thing;*
>   *now it springs forth, do you not perceive it?*
> *I will make a way in the wilderness*
>   *and rivers in the desert.*
>   ISAIAH 43:19

Cooking without Food

Imagination is more important than knowledge.
ALBERT EINSTEIN

It is Holocaust Remembrance Day, *Yom HaShoah.* Chapman University is hosting a service attended by hundreds of people of all faiths. At a dinner before the service, I am pleased to be seated at a table of survivors with stories to tell. I can hardly eat the delicious fish and fruit and pastries for fear of missing even one droplet of recollection from these beautiful souls around me. I am hearing stories that make my heart weep and my toes curl. But mostly I am hearing the story of goodness—the story of overcoming and love and healing.

Elizabeth, quiet and poised and red-haired, sits next to me on the left. She's a Polish American who survived Auschwitz at age eighteen. During our conversation I tell her I am writing a book on the power of Beauty. She says, "I like that. Beauty—in the form of imagination—actually saved my life."

My ears perked up like a cat. "Please, tell me how imagination saved you, how Beauty made a difference."

She said to me, "I used my imagination every day. I could see myself at home with my family. I could almost touch and smell and taste everything around me. And because I was so hungry, I mainly imagined food! I thought of my mother's kitchen, and of myself cooking in that kitchen—all her delicious dishes! I thought of my father, my brothers, and sister exactly as they looked, and could hear them talking and laughing. I could see the wallpaper in the bathroom and hear familiar footsteps on the stairs. I lived in this imaginary world, which was a beautiful world for me. It saved me. It strengthened me, and I survived."

I could see the images of her family as clearly as she saw them herself.

On my right were Schindler's list survivors. These folks owe their lives and their children's lives and generations to come to rescuer Oskar Schindler. I asked them if he was like the man in the film. "Yes," said one survivor, "exactly in character, but not in appearance. He surely did not *look* like Liam Neeson!"

We laughed. Their love for this man radiated from them. They had let go of revenge and hatred toward those who tried to kill them—they had to in order to survive. We talked about it. One man said, "I felt revengeful, yes, but I also knew I did not want to be like them." So having let go of hatred, all that they keep wrapped around their pain is the love for the one who saved them.

I learned that night that coping with evil can flatten one's soul or expand it to the size of the sun. These survivors had huge souls and radiant spirits that could envelope you in hope.

Before I left, Elizabeth asked, "Patricia, you are a teacher?"

"Yes, I am."

"That's marvelous. I have a message for your students. Tell them that no matter what happens to you in life, no one can ever take away your knowledge, your imagination, and your goodwill." She said this with kindness and true conviction.

"I'll tell them. Thank you, Elizabeth."

We all said good-bye, and I felt my heart would burst with gratitude.

I have given you as a covenant to the people,
  a light to the nations,
  to open the eyes that are blind,
to bring out the prisoners from the dungeon,
  from the prison those who sit in darkness.
ISAIAH 42:6–7

PART 5

Embracing Beauty in Cats and Other Creatures

The smallest feline is a masterpiece.
LEONARDO DA VINCI

Cat-A-Tonic

There are two means of refuge from the miseries of life: music and cats.

ALBERT SCHWEITZER

The best things in life are free—until you take them to the vet. On October 7, 2001, the day America began bombing Afghanistan, a box of eight-week-old kittens was dropped off anonymously at the door of my church before anyone arrived. There they were: squirming, squinty-eyed little blobs of color, whiskers, and ears, falling all over one another in a big cardboard box with a couple of cans of open cat food, and ants galore.

When the box was opened—with a crowd gathering and kittens of all colors popping their tiny heads out—one of the church members ran up to me with somber face to tell me we had begun military action in Afghanistan. But it seemed that the only thing that mattered at the moment was rescuing these helpless little creatures and getting the ants out of the box. That day the nursery of the church was turned into a little kitten nursery. Because I happened to be the minister of the church, finding a home for these little creatures became my ministerial mission for the day. If ever I had been a zealot for the homeless, it was now! These kittens were going to be saved and loved and in caring homes by nightfall, come terrorists, hell, or high water. I would see to that.

For me, it was love at first sight. I would have taken all of them if I could, but I ended up with the two leftovers. These lively green-eyed, snow-white kittens were named that very day Matisse and Monet, because they looked like works of art.

I knew our home had no room for more cats. I knew we didn't have the time or money to put into kittens. But against all these brutal facts I also knew these cats needed me and I needed them. That's all that really mattered. Holding these helpless, squirmy, little white creatures on a day of fear and uncertainty broke down any reserves of resistance. They were the most beautiful creatures I had ever seen. These little gifts from God cut through all my perceived obstacles.

Beauty has a way of undoing us.

Matisse and Monet eat like horses, claw every piece of good furniture, wrestle wildly, and pester the daylights out of our two

100

older cats. But I love them. Giving these two kittens a home and love was just the tonic I needed in the face of a growing escalation of violence in the world. In that box—on that day when we were all thinking of war—nestled life, innocence, love, and vulnerability. Something small, yet something hugely significant.

In the darkness of world events, we need such tiny, soft graces to remind us that God is still alive, that life goes on with squinty eyes, tender care, and resilience. When these two bright snowflakes descended from heaven on a day of war, I knew that everything would be all right if there is still this Beauty to treasure and care for.

White kittens falling from heaven on the doorstep of my church on a day when all the fears of war came tumbling down, I knew this to be a divine thing. I knew by this rescue, however small in the scheme of things, that God needs me now more than ever. Beauty must be rescued and protected, especially during war! Rather than retreat in fear or deny our connection to such faraway events in apathetic disregard, we need to go ahead and look at what our world is about, feel it, see it for what it is, and offer ourselves to be caretakers of Beauty in the midst of it all.

I do believe God sends us such reminder gifts, that Love and Beauty are ultimately indestructible. We just need to look for these boxes of hope on the doorsteps of our days.

> *"For I was hungry and you gave me food, I was thirsty and you gave me something to drink, I was a stranger and you welcomed me."*
> MATTHEW 25:35

Friends of the Sea Lions

A friend at one's back is a safe bridge.
DUTCH SAYING

I remember an episode of *Seinfeld* in which a beached whale provides an opportunity for all-around loser George Costanza to pretend he's a marine biologist to impress his girlfriend. Despite George's idiotic rouse, the whale survives, but the jig is up, and

George is in trouble again. I don't think George had too much empathy for sea creatures. But I'm glad some people do.

Walking down the beach on this clear, soft morning, when the waves are high enough to be a surfer's dream and the ocean is as blue as my cat's eyes, I wish for a brief time that I were a marine biologist. I come across a group of folks who are gathering in excitement. I assume they see a dolphin near the shore and I join the crowd. But it's a baby seal—a pup—struggling in the rough, frothy surf. A couple of times he makes it onto the shore with his small, sleek, dark body shining in the sun. But of course, with all the gawking onlookers, including me, he's too scared and falls back into the heavy sea.

We all want to help this small, lost creature from the sea. But we're not helping at all. Children are screaming in excitement; cameras are flashing; and a surfer goes in for a closer look. The surfer comes back reporting that the poor thing is gasping for air, so much you can hear it. We want to help, but we're doing everything wrong.

I pull out my cell phone ready to call anyone, 911 if necessary. I ask around. The surfer suggests calling Friends of the Sea Lions. I call them. They ask questions, and I do my best to give answers. "It's a harbor seal," they conclude. They tell me to get the folks away from the seal so it won't be frightened. I'm not very good at things like this—but I do my best. Despite my efforts, the pup disappears in the dizzy, white froth, even while I'm talking, and the crowd disperses with their pictures ready for the one-hour photo special.

The seal is gone for now. End of story.

But no. The Friends of the Sea Lions come anyway. Not just one friend, but *four* Friends of the Sea Lions arrive within minutes. They assure me that if the seal is sick, he will beach himself in a quiet place, and then they can take over from there—all in due process. They care—I can see that. They watch and wait for the little black head to bob up out of the waves. Although he doesn't surface again while I am present, I go away feeling comforted that there are such people in the world called Friends of the Sea Lions. My heart still hurts for the seal, but I feel better about humanity.

Feeling helpless is our lot in so many instances. Seeing a loved one or an animal hurting and not knowing what to do has to be one of the worst feelings possible. We want to make sure the best possible care is at hand. That's what friends do. But as I learned from this tiny, shiny, confused creature, we have to be careful that we don't crowd and suffocate a person with our desperate need to fix things. Suffering animals or people are frightened–scared out of their wits. They need to know that they have friends who love them, but they have to go through the grief or the pain themselves. There is a process. They need time. They may not be able to just "get over it." They need space. We may need to back off and let them be, knowing that timing is everything.

If I had been a marine biologist, I would have already known all this. But because I am a mere bystander, I can learn something about seals and about friendship. And about God.

Psychologist Robert Brizee suggests that we image God as Caring Friend, and I see that here in this place. God, like the Friends of the Sea Lions, does not force or crowd or automatically fix things. God works patiently, gently, to lure us to shore so we can find the healing we need. God is always waiting for us, even in our suffering, even when we feel frightened and confused. When we're floundering in the strong current, we are not lost, but just waiting for someone to give us room to heal and be healed.

Our friend of the universe waits patiently on the shore.

A friend loves at all times.
PROVERBS 17:17

When God Sighs

Hope is a thing with feathers
that perches in the soul
and sings the tune
without the words
and never stops at all.

EMILY DICKINSON

Way up in the eaves of my front porch lives an insane bird. Her enormous, frightened eyes peek down at me every morning. And every morning I find her nest fallen onto the concrete porch. And each day I take my broom to sweep up the strewn nest.

Every day it falls down and scatters, and every day I sweep up the mess.

Apparently it has not dawned on her that there's no room for a nest in the eaves of my front porch. I find it annoying, of course, and begin to mentally implore the bird to move on. But the twigs keep coming, the nest keeps falling, and I keep sweeping.

But then one morning I find a broken egg on top of the strewn nest. The next day, another broken egg. Then I realize how sad it is to never learn from your mistakes.

And every morning I look into her eyes and sigh.

When I think about this bird, who is very likely never to have any offspring under my eaves, I wonder how God must do a great deal of sighing and suffering as a result of our insanity.

I've heard it said that the definition of insanity is doing the same thing over and over and expecting different results. And in this insanity so much is broken, splattered, and swept away!

And God sighs.

God is deeply touched by our sufferings, our insanity, and our goodness too. I feel so deeply for this bird and her troubles. God feels her frustration much more intimately than I do. That's because in Beauty's world, there is a divine presence in every experience, even in a falling egg.

And in this intricately woven world in which everything matters, from falling eggs to falling bombs, there is this Beauty—this compassionate, divine Beauty that feels and sighs and understands.

But God's sigh is more than compassion. Within this divine sigh that is "too deep for words" we hear the beginning of a melody of hope. It is a new melody, a new thing, a new offering of possibility. Oh, how we need to hear this melody of hope when our efforts keep crashing like eggs in falling nests! When people are blown to bits in war, like splattering eggs on the porch, a divine anguish echoes throughout creation. But it is always followed with a melody of hope. Always.

I wish I could give this bird hope. But perhaps she is listening to the divine melody that she knows, a melody that calls her to some new place where her nest will not fall and her eggs will hatch safely.

A new thing is not always good news. This bird does not want to leave. We don't like change either. It may be a tremendous risk to go outside our comfort zone—a flight into unfamiliar territory. But if we know that God's presence is the one constant we have in our lives, we can fly off to a new place or begin building a safer world in which eggs and people are not broken by insanity.

And God's sigh is transposed into a new key, a melody of hope that is carried by the wind of the Spirit to all the places and peoples and creatures that need so desperately to hear a new song.

> *"Are not two sparrows sold for a penny? Yet not one of them will fall to the ground apart from your Father."*
> MATTHEW 10:29

Hidden in Plain Sight

One should lie empty, open, choiceless as a beach—waiting for a gift from the sea.

ANNE MORROW LINDBERGH

He's digging for something. The sleek brown dog on the sun-drenched beach catches my eye—sand flying, tail wagging; the poor dog just keeps digging. What a shame, I think, this dog digging a hole in the sand for no apparent reason. While he is digging madly, seemingly intoxicated with a passion for finding something, another almost identical brown dog sits nearby staring into the ocean, alert and watchful.

Their human companion then throws an object into the waves, and the sitting dog flies after it, crashing through the rolling breakers with abandon, catching the object just before it hits the water. Hooray!

But then I look again at the other dog digging himself deeper into the empty sand. If only he knew that the object of his desire is hidden in plain sight. If only he could look up for a second from his mad digging! All his energies are spent digging, when what he really needs to do is sit and watch and expect.

Mary and Martha come to mind, one sitting at the feet of Jesus, one busying herself into an irritable outburst. I wonder how much useless energy we spend searching for things, for answers, for happiness, for Beauty. For God. We think we have to dig deeper and deeper, but all the while we're digging ourselves into a hole of anxiety or "analysis paralysis."

We often find ourselves trying too hard, looking down when we need to look up, narrowing our view and thereby blocking out the world in which a beautiful God is glistening on top of the sea. And a beautiful God *is* the object of our true desire. We are wired for God, who is the source of all things good and beautiful. But we are so busy digging for other things that we miss out on the joy of this tender Presence in our lives.

Sometimes we need to pray by *opening* our eyes to what is around us—people we love, stars in the night, birds dipping gracefully to the surface of the sea. We need to be looking for God and Beauty in our daily lives, opening up to the hidden God who is present in the sparkling water, the ocean breeze, the sand castle, and the crab. When the objects of our desire are flung by grace into our lives, we need to be ready to catch them before they disappear into the deep. Rather than digging ourselves into a hole with worry or busyness or obsession over a problem, we need simply to open our eyes to the divine answers that come to us in the world around us.

God is hidden in plain sight. This God who knows all our deepest desires is ready to be unveiled in the dailiness of life. Look for God today in everything that sparkles with Life and Beauty. Let your anxieties, your longings, and your heartbreaks wash into the vast sea of this welcoming, healing Presence.

Take a lesson from two dogs, one who is exhausted and frustrated from digging impatiently, and one who sits and watches, capturing his dream on an ocean of delight.

But Martha was distracted by her many tasks.
Luke 10:40

Out, Damned Spot!

Guilt: the gift that keeps on giving.
Erma Bombeck

If I could choose any manner of death, I would choose to die in a huge vat of chocolate. From the way I like to cook with it, you'd think I was on my way. Mimi, my pretty seal-point rag-doll cat, is my coconspirator in chocolate madness. Not that she eats it. Chocolate is not good for cats. Mimi, always perfectly groomed and proper, just likes to watch me make messes. From a distance.

Cats are good company. They are a revelation to our human egotism. Cats remind us—in not-so-subtle ways—that we are not the center of the universe.

On a lazy Sunday afternoon, Mimi and I go to work in the kitchen. I melt a pound of dark chocolate in which to dip plump Turkish apricots. Mimi's job is to sit on a kitchen chair and look beautiful while I work. Mimi takes great interest as I carefully dip each apricot and place it on the waxed paper. Then one for me. Then one for the waxed paper...one for me...She cranes her neck a bit to see the chocolate dripping all over the cabinet, all over my clothes, all over my face. It's messy. It's the way I do things, and Mimi loves it.

But today Mimi is feeling the need for some close-up inspection of the apricots. She suddenly jumps up on the cabinet right smack in the middle of the still-soft chocolate apricots.

"Mimi! Get down!" Thinking only of my apricots, I grab Mimi with both of my chocolate-covered hands. Her creamy white fur is suddenly soiled with chocolate handprints. Mimi is quite fussy about personal hygiene and grooming, so this sudden chocolate abomination has her reeling. She is understandably put off by the whole chocolate mess and refuses to let me wipe if off of her before it hardens into permanent handprints. Instead, she catapults off the cabinet, darts around like a squirrel, and meows something that sounds to me like "Out, out, damned spot!"

Now the question is, what do you do with a chocolate-covered cat? There's not much you can do. She's a cat. She has her own mind—her own ways of dealing with such catastrophes—and human opinion bears no weight at all. If she wants to run around like a squirrel and be upset over the horrible violation of her personal hygiene, then so be it.

Mimi's mistake makes me ponder over the mistakes I make in life when I jump into the wrong place at the wrong time. Maybe it's saying the wrong thing or making a rash decision that I know is wrong even as I am making it. I may get into things that are not so good for me and wonder why I feel so icky. When we mess up, we often try to escape in a panic, rushing from here to there to hide the visible signs of pain and anguish all over our faces. People can tell that we're not quite the same.

Something is different. We feel out of sorts and uncomfortable and would like to just be rid of this mistake, like Lady Macbeth, but it's stuck on us like glue.

What do we do when we feel like a chocolate-covered cat? Maybe we can learn from the experience never to jump in before we know what in the world we're jumping into. We can also learn that if we just sit still long enough in prayer, we can give God a chance to brush out the icky stuff and help restore that shiny coat again. Running around like a squirrel quoting Shakespeare will not help get the chocolate off. The worst part of doing something wrong is the guilt that we carry with us like chocolate handprints. But sitting still in the peace of prayer and quiet meditation might just help us make peace with ourselves and God.

We know that no matter how much we mess up or how much we are violated by the messes of others, God's Beauty will restore us and make us whole. We are beloved, beautiful creatures who happen to have chocolate on us. It is not for forever. We will not be thrown to the dogs for our mistakes. There is always healing, forgiveness. And, of course, baths.

Robert Brizee, author of *Eight Paths to Forgiveness,* says,

God forgives us in each new split second; that is, God is present with a lure lovingly offered that is the most enriching possibility both for us and for all creation...Such is grace: The divine gives to us without reference to whether or not we deserve it. The Presence accompanies us regardless of what we do.[1]

The Presence he speaks of sees our Beauty underneath the messy mistakes. If we're covered with chocolate by our own blunderings or by the hands of another, we need to know that Beauty is there to restore us. We need not suffer more than necessary. As the saying goes, pain and suffering in life are inevitable, but misery is optional.

Learn a lesson from Mimi and walk gently over the chocolate-covered apricots of life.

Wash me thoroughly from my iniquity.
    PSALM 51:2

---

[1]Robert Brizee, *Eight Paths to Forgiveness* (St. Louis: Chalice Press, 1998), 125.

The Truth about Birds

But in the real world it is more important that a proposition
be interesting than that it be true.

ALFRED NORTH WHITEHEAD

I'm walking past a soccer field where, on most weekends, little people in bright uniforms kick a ball around while big people scream much too loudly. (That's all I know about soccer.) But today all is quiet, almost eerie. No noisy parents, bright uniforms, or excited coaches in sight. Instead, the field is covered with seagulls, one right after another, lined up in ghostly silence. Are they praying? There must be twenty-five or thirty birds, all snow white, with their eyes toward the California sun. They are almost like angels–or maybe aliens in bird attire, awaiting their ship to carry them home.

I know even less about ornithology than I do about soccer. But I do know that some of the greatest theologians and philosophers, including Charles Hartshorne, were bird lovers. Birds evoke a special sense of the holy within us. These mysterious creatures are even linked genetically to the dinosaurs.

Snow-white birds–halted, still, unmoved in silent communion–speak to me of the holy. What are they doing? Going back to my very first thought, they *must* be praying. Is this a naive notion? If it is, then perhaps that is good news. Sometimes we get so caught up in debates about the "truth" of things that we lose the Truth in the moment. What we have figured out with our historical and scientific studies may not be the whole truth. Bible stories are lightning rods for debate on this issue of truth. Whether these imaginative stories are historically verifiable or have scientific veracity is surely of interest to some, but it is what they evoke within us that brings us into the Holy Presence. Every tradition–from Native American cosmology to the colorful stories of seraphs in Isaiah–is full of stories that may not be "true," but they unfold within our souls as Truth.

Birds who line up for morning prayers may not be true in an ornithological sense. They don't have brains as we do. But I do believe they pray, for they are as much a part of God as we are. They are listening to the divine Breathing in the universe and responding with their God-given instincts and with whatever level of awareness they possess.

And to us, it is graceful mystery.

These creatures of our unknowing glide over the sea's deep mysteries, charm our mornings with song, and lure our imaginations upward toward new possibilities. So then, can we set aside our learned baggage for a moment and simply see the world through the eyes of a grace-filled God in whose bosom all creatures thrive?

One of those great theologians I spoke of who loved birds was Will Beardslee. During his memorial service, Will's son remarked of his father: "He saw grace everywhere." Maybe we could find this same magical grace in our lives if we looked at birds as Will did, not as just birds but as winged storytellers that lure us into an unfathomable sky of Beauty's imagination. They are showing us how to be still and how to be free and how to pray. They remind us to see grace everywhere.

And that's the truth!

> *"Are not five sparrows sold for two pennies? Yet not one of them is forgotten in God's sight."*
> LUKE 12:6

Moving with the Sun

All creation is gifted with the ecstasy of God's light.
HILDEGARD OF BINGEN

Nekay stretches out on the carpet, his tabby yellow softness creating a striking study in chiaroscuro—sunlit gold against the emerald green carpet. This is an everyday scene around our house. But I notice something today. It's not just his lazy, step-over-me-I'm-not-moving pose that catches my attention. What I find inspiring in my chubby, yellow friend is *where* on the carpet he chooses to sleep. He picks the one spot where the sun hits the carpet, regardless of the fact that it is directly in the middle of everyone's way. That means lazy Nekay has to get up enough energy to move every now and then in order to keep up with the gently moving sun. His hair glistens like warm honey in the gorgeous light, so I tolerate stepping over him in my comings and goings just to fill my soul with the sun on Nekay's fur.

As I watch Nekay's whiskers twitch and gleam in the sleepy sun, I realize that he's not so much lazy as just plain smart. Following the sun keeps Nekay in the warmth and comfort he is made for. Nekay simply loves light and warmth, and he knows that following the sun will bring him the most satisfaction.

Light is a wonderful metaphor for God, found both in the Hebrew Bible and in the New Testament. From the burning bush to the star of Bethlehem, God is light. If we want to be in the Light, we need to be with it wherever it is, always attentive to its gentle movements.

If we want to bask in God and find the contentment Nekay has found in the sun, we need to follow the gentle movements of God each moment of the day. Being stuck in one spot may leave us cold. We need to move with the Spirit and find the warmth and radiance in the movement of God. We need to study the Light and let our mission in life be to be in the center of it, in the center of God's light. It is there that we will find happiness, love, and our true destiny.

We often think of God as static and of the Bible as rigid and one-dimensional. But the truth is, this Light is always moving forward, luring us tenderly toward all that is good and true and beautiful. And in this gentle movement, the Spirit never ceases to bring forth fresh morning light in each day's adventures, in each experience, and in the pages of the Bible—which is itself alive!

Follow the wisdom of Nekay. Move with the sun. Be attentive to where the Light of God is shining in each part of the day, and go there. It may mean laughing out loud in the morning and sitting with a friend in grief in the afternoon. Wherever you sense the Light is, be with it, right in the center of it, and you'll always find warmth and joy

How do you know which way the Light is moving? You'll know because it emanates from deep within you. You'll know because Light is made up of love, peace, justice, and well-being for all creation. Follow these, and you'll always be in the warmth of Beauty's radiance.

In him was life, and the life was the light of all people.
JOHN 1:4

One Cool Cat

Common sense is not so common.

VOLTAIRE

You know you have too many cats when they start popping out of the refrigerator. I was mortified one Sunday afternoon when I came home from church famished and opened the fridge only to find one cool cat sitting on the shelf between the celery and the cucumbers.

Thankfully Monet was unhurt and went blissfully off to play with brother Matisse as if nothing were wrong, as if it were perfectly natural to snooze in the refrigerator on a Sunday morning. I, however, practically suffered a heart attack. I'm just glad I didn't lollygag on the way home or stop off for lunch at some busy buffet. The oxygen level is limited in that space, but—thank goodness!—I have a super duper sized fridge to accommodate large casseroles and a cat or two for several hours.

Now the really strange thing about this incident is that Monet continues trying his best to jump into the fridge. You would think that after hours of cramping cold the cat would learn. But Monet will not learn. He wants to be in the fridge, on any shelf—he's not particular. And since his color—white—matches the fridge, it's a challenge sometimes to see the critter at all.

Not long after this, my husband and I were on a trip to see friends but had to return halfway there because I'd failed to check the fridge for cats before we left. Checking the fridge for cats has become a usual ritual at our house, like checking the lights or making sure the stove is turned off.

Pea-brained—that's what cats are.

But are we any different? I wonder how our loved ones must be befuddled over our own actions that take us into states of mind that are as cold and dark and cramped as a refrigerator. You would think we would learn after one bad incident. We may decide one day to cramp ourselves into a tiny hole of self-pity even as we realize we are making ourselves utterly miserable—and everyone else around us as well. You'd think one stretch of such nonsense would cure us. Logically, we should run at the thought of lonely self-pity or cramping fear because we know how miserable and unproductive it is.

But no, we keep going back there, to that dark, damp, cold, cramped mind-set, like a silly cat with a pea-sized brain. We jump into that little space—just for a moment—and the door closes on us, and before we know it we're locked into sheer dread as dark and cold as we ever imagined. And the longer we are in there, the less we can breathe.

Whatever we are tempted to do or think or obsess over, we don't seem to learn, even when we *know* that the place we are going is cold and dark and lonely. We have a hard time breaking down the heavy, incessant power of the past. It wants to repeat itself, as if we are doomed to continue doing the same thing forever, like Sisyphus pushing the same boulder up the hill only to have it roll right back down again. For eternity.

There is liberation from all this nonsense. We are not destined to repeat the past. The reason why we are not destined to a cycle of refrigerator madness or endless boulder pushing is because of Beauty's creative, transforming power. Our beautiful God always offers something novel in the midst of the heavy, weighty past. God is that part of our experience that can empower us into a new way of making choices that are not so utterly pea-brained.

"The worst mistake we can make is to fence in our possibilities," says cosmologist Brian Swimme. We need to believe in creative possibilities if we are to survive. It's that simple.

God's Beauty is many things; empowerment to change is one of them. Freedom from past cycles of misery—whether they are the larger catastrophes of violence or our own personal demons—is a possibility that only we can realize. This empowering Presence is with us even in the cold, dark, and lonely imprisonments of our deepest yearnings.

Even cats, despite their silly habits, are capable of experiencing God's lure toward something better. God's Beauty can liberate our true desires into much more interesting and lively and delicious places than a refrigerator. It is a power that is tender and warm and more alluring than anything else imaginable.

There is something beautiful afoot in the world. Believe in it. Embrace it, and never ever let it go.

One thing I asked of the LORD,
* that will I seek after:*
to live in the house of the LORD
* all the days of my life,*
to behold the beauty of the LORD.
            PSALM 27:4

🐾

EPILOGUE

Just One More Thing

The teleology of the Universe is directed to the production of Beauty.

ALFRED NORTH WHITEHEAD

This is our destiny: To awaken the creativity of the Universe.

BRIAN SWIMME

Beauty is the end to which we must all strive and hope and dream. For this one thing, I believe, is descriptive of God's own purpose for the world.

But just one more thing.

I am not alone in my vision of God. What I am saying is a result of my embrace of a beautiful way of viewing the world. This worldview is called "process theology."

Process thought from the writings of mathematician and cosmologist Alfred North Whitehead (1861–1947) has liberated and enchanted my deepest philosophical longings.

Whitehead's religious thought has been creatively developed by the late professor Charles Hartshorne and by my own mentors and friends from the Claremont Graduate School and School of Theology: philosopher David Ray Griffin; theologians John B. Cobb, Jr., and Marjorie Hewitt Suchocki; and the late biblical scholar William A. Beardslee. These visionary scholars have developed the Center for Process Studies and the Process and Faith Program at Claremont. People from all over the world, from every religious tradition and walk of life, come to this graceful place to learn of process thought.[1]

---

[1] For more information and further reading on process theology, go to the Process and Faith Web site (www.processandfaith.org) or write to Process and Faith, 1325 North College Avenue, Claremont, CA 91711.

115

Many process thinkers are not formal theologians at all, but are physicists, biologists, philosophers, teachers, writers, economists, artists, and ecologists. That's because this beautiful vision of the world is much bigger than any one particular corner. You see, Whitehead was a cosmologist. Cosmology means big. Huge. All-encompassing. Cosmology is a picture of the universe and how we fit in. Cosmology is not just science but the interweaving of science, philosophy, art, and religion. Whitehead's cosmology—his picture of the universe—is interdependent, gorgeous, divinely inhabited, evolving, moving always toward that which is beautiful.

While many of us have zeroed in on how Whitehead's cosmology can transform our theology—and maybe even our faith communities—we must never lose sight of this grand scheme of things—the way the universe unfolds into ever more complex and wondrous adventures. The organic cosmology offered by Whitehead speaks to all people of every faith and no faith. We need to keep the big picture always before us—the way primal peoples, Buddhists, and Native Americans have always believed—that we are organically involved with one another and with cats and ladybugs and rocks and stars. And that we breathe in the molecules of all humankind each time we inhale.

Whitehead's *Process and Reality* was my "blood, sweat, and tears" in graduate school; it is a daunting read with a whole language in and unto itself. But it is truly a masterpiece in thought and execution. Today we hear similar voices bringing forth this organic view of things. The cosmology of Brian Swimme, mathematical cosmologist at the California Institute for Integral Studies, echoes Whitehead's organic notions of reality when he speaks of music in rocks and dragonflies who keep us in their watch. Swimme reverberates the Beauty of Einstein and Whitehead, but with his own fresh contributions of genius, poetic vision, and spiritual insights.

Don't be afraid to delve into the big picture. Think big thoughts. Do not just embrace Beauty. *Be embraced.* Let the whole grasp you in its mystery and hold you spellbound with divine possibilities! The future of our species and our planet depends on this larger vision. Allow yourself some room to be surprised and bedazzled by an unfolding universe that welcomes you into its celebration. You are a significant part of this ongoing cosmic story.

You have a place in the universe.

Whether we are Christian or Buddhist or Jewish or Muslim or of any other faith tradition, if we are truly a part of one another's breath, then we can breathe into a deeper, wider, welcoming universe in which everyone belongs and everyone is beautiful.

Finally, my wish and blessing for all my readers:

That you embrace the beautiful in each moment:
Dancing in the shining radiance of God's Beauty.
Holding gently all the strands of your experience.
Offering bouquets of creativity to God and to the world.
Venturing forth into your deepest yearnings.
Balancing Harmony and Freshness.
Opening your eyes and ears to the Whole.
Treasuring all that is life-bearing with gratitude.
Letting go to the Divine flow of Creative, Transforming Love.
Kissing the earth and finding your place among the stars.

INDEX OF QUOTED AUTHORS

INDEX OF SCRIPTURES

INDEX OF THEMES